I0454687

EIR (ISSN 0273-6314) *is published weekly
(50 issues), by EIR News Service, Inc.,
P.O. Box 17390, Washington, D.C. 20041-0390.
(703) 777-9451 ext. 415*

European Headquarters: E.I.R. GmbH, Postfach
Bahnstrasse 9a, D-65205, Wiesbaden, Germany
Tel: 49-611-73650
Homepage: http://www.eirna.com
e-mail: eirna@eirna.com
Director: Georg Neudecker

Montreal, Canada: 514-461-1557

Denmark: EIR - Danmark, Sankt Knuds Vej 11,
basement left, DK-1903 Frederiksberg, Denmark.
Tel.: +45 35 43 60 40, Fax: +45 35 43 87 57. e-mail:
eirdk@hotmail.com.

Mexico City: EIR, Sor Juana Inés de la Cruz 242-2
Col. Agricultura C.P. 11360
Delegación M. Hidalgo, México D.F.
Tel. (5525) 5318-2301
eirmexico@gmail.com

Canada Post Publication Sales Agreement
#40683579

Postmaster: Send all address changes to *EIR*, P.O.
Box 17390, Washington, D.C. 20041-0390.

Signed articles in *EIR* represent the views of the
authors, and not necessarily those of the Editorial
Board.

The Einstein Era

EIRContents

www.larouchepub.com Volume 43, Number 34, August 19, 2016

NASA

I. Our Task at This Moment in History

EUROPE OUT OF STEP WITH THE ZEITGEIST

The New Silk Road Shows the Way!

by Helga Zepp-LaRouche

The author is chairwoman of the Civil Rights Solidarity Movement party (BüSo) in Germany.

Aug. 13—The establishments in the various European countries—one can't call them elites—are currently confronted with a wide array of impressions that they obviously haven't come to terms with yet. To come to the point: Europeans who are stuck in the old Eurocentric mode of thinking are experiencing a clash between their ideology and reality. The so-called "mainstream" politicians and media are lamenting the growing number of crises—Brexit, the EU and Euro crisis, the banking crisis, the flood of refugees, terrorism, anti-globalization movements—with no capability or readiness to recognize and deal with their own false assumptions that have contributed to these crises, or even to correct them.

We are currently experiencing the process of change to a totally new strategic alignment, in which the center of gravity has long since shifted to Asia, where a new alliance network, bound together with a common vision of the future, is developing. Almost three years late, several financial publications have discovered that China, with its program for a New Silk Road, has brought about a perspective for development embracing 64 countries and 4.4 billion people, which in absolute

European Union Headquarters in Brussels, Belgium.

dollar amounts ($1.2 trillion) is 12 times larger than the Marshall Plan in today's purchasing power, and which already includes 40 percent of the world economy.

"The fact that this is a 30-40 year plan is remarkable, as China is the only country with any long-term development plan, and this underscores the policy long-termism in China, in contrast to the dominance of policy short-termism in the West," former IMF economist Stephen L. Jen told *Bloomberg* in an interview August 7.

In contrast to China, the results of a study by the McKinsey Global Institute show that the living standards of 70 percent of the population in the 25 most important industrialized countries shrank from 2005 to 2014, and that future generations are threatened with growing impoverishment. Meanwhile, China had freed 600 million of its people from poverty between 1981 and 2008, helping them to reach a good standard of living, and the process has continued ever since.

Despite this blatant discrepancy, the politicians and media in Europe totally ignore this divergent dynamic. After his participation in the conference of the Shanghai Cooperation Organization (SCO) in Tashkent—a meeting scarcely mentioned in the Western media—British historian Peter Frankopan, author of the book, *The Silk Roads: A New History of the World*, commented on Europe's in-

Grand Design for stabilizing the entire Central Asian region: (clockwise from above) Russian President Vladimir Putin (right) shaking hands with President of Armenia Serzh Sargsyan at a joint news conference in the Kremlin, Aug. 10, 2016; President Putin and Kazakhstan President Nursultan Nazurbayev; President Putin (right), Azerbaijan President Ilham Aliyev (center) and Iran President Hassan Rouhani (left), before the start of a trilateral meeting Aug. 8, 2016; President Putin at a news conference in St. Petersburg, Russia, with Turkish President Recep Tayyip Erdogan, following talks on Aug. 9, 2016.

difference: "Our focus in Europe has resulting in us missing the total picture. We are living with our totally wrong perception, and have lost our connection to reality."

Building the World

This future-oriented dynamic, China's policy of the New Silk Road, the new financial system of the Asian Infrastructure Investment Bank (AIIB), the New Development Bank, the Silk Road Fund, and more—all based on the real economy—, the new strategic alliances between the BRICS and the SCO, the strategic partnership between China and Russia: All of these ele-

ments were the backdrop to the rapprochement between Russian President Putin and Turkish President Erdogan, which was in the making months *before* the coup attempt in Turkey. As early as 2013, when Erdogan was prime minister, he noted that Turkey was frustrated by its futile efforts to join the EU and was attempting to join the SCO, because the SCO was "better, stronger, and would yield more mutual results."

The unanimity with which the West sided with the coup plotters in Turkey, while Putin immediately supported the democratically elected Erdogan government, contributed to that attitude. During Erdogan's recent visit to St. Petersburg, not only were important economic agreements concluded between Russia and Turkey—on matters such as the construction of the Turkish Stream natural gas pipeline, agricultural exports, tourism, and the construction of a nuclear power plant—but there was a strategically decisive arrangement for acting together in Syria against the Islamic State and other terrorist organizations. All thinking Europeans immediately welcomed this collaboration as a *sine qua non*.

Meanwhile Putin has been working on a Grand Design for stabilizing the entire Central Asian region through an array of summit meetings with the heads of state of Iran, Azerbaijan, and Armenia, and the agreement on the International North-South Transportation Corridor from Europe to India, through Russia, Azerbaijan, and Iran.

Enrico Letta, Italian prime minister 2013-2014: "The European Union must go back to the beginning and start over, or else go under." No Maastricht austerity, no Euro. Photo from the Festival dell'Economia di Trento, 2013.

Thinking Inside the Box

While Asian nations have worked out the construction of an entirely new model of economic cooperation, the European regimes and institutions have insisted on a policy that is as useless as it is arrogant: "Let's have more of the same!" That is, more "unconventional monetary measures" such as Quantitative Easing, negative interest rates, and helicopter money, and more austerity, and more globalization—although all of these policy measures have been hopelessly discredited.

All the more interesting, therefore, that certain representatives of the Establishment, such as, Paul Goldschmidt, a former Goldman Sachs banker, have come forward with urgent warnings that the system of universal banking must be replaced with a system of bank separation (such as Glass-Steagall). Otherwise, he says, the threatened collapse of the banking system will not only have the most severe economic and social consequences, but will also threaten to shatter the foundations of the European democracies. Under universal banking, the fundamental conflict between the interests of depositors and borrowers inevitably comes to

Li Zhaoxing, former foreign minister of China, who spoke in Singapore, Aug. 16, said the New Silk Road is "a broad road shared by all" for win-win outcomes. "China has no geostrategic intention of seeking the so-called sphere of influence," he said.

a head. Only the immediate introduction of Glass-Steagall banking separation can defuse this explosive situation. And this from a former Goldman Sachs banker!

Economist Joseph Stiglitz is another member of the chorus of those to whom the quote from Schiller applies, "He comes late, yet he comes!"—from *Wallensteins Tod* (Wallenstein's Death). In his new book, *The Euro: How a Common Currency Threatens the Future of Europe*, Stiglitz has come to the realization that the Euro was born with a birth defect and its collapse is inevitable. Yet, if you look, you can find in my own writings, even from before the introduction of the Euro, the projection that it would not function. Nonetheless, Stiglitz is right in his assessment that the Euro has led to neither the prosperity nor integration of the Eurozone, and that the European Union can only save itself if it gives up the Euro. Obviously his proposal to introduce a "flexible Euro" is way behind the curve of rapid developments.

Symptomatic of the end phase of the trans-Atlantic financial system are the various forecasts that Deutsche Bank must ultimately be "nationalized." But that would only delay a systemic collapse, rather than stop it, which requires a change of the *policies* of Deutsche Bank—that is, orienting it again to the real economy and getting out of derivatives speculation. You can vividly imagine the joy of the German taxpayer if faced with coughing up with 19 billion euro for the immediate rescue of Deutsche Bank, with its 55 billion euro of outstanding derivatives contracts.

A Vision for a Thriving Europe

Former Italian Prime Minister Enrico Letta senses the seriousness of the situation, and has made a turn with this appeal to the public: "The EU must go back to the beginning and start over, or else go under," an appeal in which he expresses his horror at the disunity and passivity of the heads of state in the face of the EU's existential crisis. He demands statecraft rather than bureaucracy, and says that Europe can not simply be the Europe of the winners of globalization, but must protect its citizens. Hear, hear!

What happens in the coming weeks will be decisive as to whether Europe is able to survive. Fortunately the nations of Europe are not defined by the failed Maastricht-EU model and the even more disastrous model of the European currency union, which Germany, for geopolitical reasons, was forced to adopt as the price for reunification. An upcoming series of international conferences provides the framework in which an orderly reorganization of the world economic and financial system can be accomplished—the G20 Summit in Hangzhou under the chairmanship of China at the beginning of September; the economic summit in Vladivostok, also in early September, on the integration of the Eurasian Economic Union with the New Silk Road, potentially creating a common economic space from the Atlantic to the Pacific; and the BRICS summit in India in October.

The alternative is therefore before us: Germany and Europe must reorganize their bankrupt financial and banking system, and then cooperate on world reconstruction according to the New Silk Road perspective.

To succeed in this, we must all expand our horizons and think outside the European box, confront ourselves honestly with the question as to why we got into this crisis, and open up for ourselves the vision that lies before us through cooperation with the New Silk Road. In the spirit of Friedrich Schiller: You can all contribute something to this goal!

Putin's Turkish March Towards A New Security Architecture

by David Christie

The author is a member of the LaRouche PAC Policy Committee.

Aug. 16—At the United Nations General Assembly in September 2015—the year of the 70th anniversary of the the the UN's founding, only months after the defeat of fascism and the end of World War II—Vladimir Putin proposed that the nations of the world come together to create a coalition against terrorism. He said:

> On the basis of international law, we must join efforts to address the problems that all of us are facing and create a genuinely broad international coalition against terrorism.
>
> Similar to the anti-Hitler coalition, it could unite a broad range of forces that are resolutely resisting those who, just like the Nazis, sow evil and hatred of humankind. And, naturally, the Muslim countries are to play a key role in the coalition, even more so because, not only does the Islamic State pose a direct threat to them, but it also desecrates one of the greatest world religions by its bloody crimes.

A week after Putin's offer was met with silence, Ankara was rocked by suicide bomb blasts that ripped through a peace rally, killing 103 people. Weeks later, 224 people died when Metrojet Flight 9268 was downed, killing all on board, most of them Russians returning from vacations in Sharm El-Sheikh, Egypt. Then came Brussels, Paris, Orlando, and Nice—not to mention the daily horror show in population centers throughout the Middle East and North Africa. The political "leadership" and mainstream media of the trans-Atlantic community has told us that this is now the "new normal."

Normalizing terrorism as an accepted phenomenon of life is a form of insanity. Anyone serious about shaping the New Presidency and its security policy will reject this form of insanity and embrace President Vladimir Putin's offer of collaboration to form an international coalition against terrorism. Furthermore, anyone serious about shaping the New Presidency and its security policy will "know thine enemy," and tell the truth about who and what is the real force behind global terrorism, which is deployed for geopolitical aims by the British Empire. Finally, anyone serious about shaping the New Presidency and its security policy, will recognize the integrated nature of security and economic development, and will accept the repeated offers of President Xi Jinping for collaboration around China's "One Belt, One Road" program, while seeking to extend that concept to all nations.

For more than 25 years, Lyndon LaRouche and his

kremlin.ru

Russian President Vladimir Putin (left) and China's President Xi Jinping at Russian-Chinese talks on Sept. 3, 2015 in Beijing.

Helga Zepp-LaRouche on the coast of China, at Lianyungang, the "Eastern Terminal of the Eurasian Land-Bridge," where she's being interviewed by Chinese journalists in 1997.

wife and collaborator, Helga Zepp-LaRouche, have created the pathway for a World Land-Bridge based on the idea of the Silk Road, to provide a new security architecture within which all nations can move forward based on the principle of the "advantage of the other." The leadership of Russia and China are moving forward in this direction, and Putin's latest collaborative efforts in Turkey are a case in point.

Putin's Turkish March

Putin's recent moves in Turkey indicate the nature of the new security architecture that is now being discussed on the planet, and that should be a central feature of the New Presidency immediately. Putin's actions over the course of this last year, since the United Nations General Assembly, have shown a powerful mastery of a strategic situation which is completely unprecedented in human history, and the complex relations with Turkey are a prime example. In November of last year, Putin showed intense restraint and awareness of the nature of the provocation, when Turkey shot down a Russian fighter jet. Erdogan not only refused to apologize, but continued to allow ISIS and Al-Nusra (Al-Qaeda) jihadists to use Turkish territory for transit and logistics, even in the face of Russian evidence of Turkey's illicit role in supporting terrorist networks.

Erdogan was also very close to Obama, who was organizing the anti-Russian policy from the top.

In June of this year, the situation shifted dramatically. Erdogan apologized to Putin for the incident involving the downed fighter jet and also announced his and Putin's intention for a face-to-face meeting. On cue, terrorists killed 45 people and wounded 230 at the Istanbul Airport the next day. Lyndon LaRouche pointed to the Chechen role in the terrorist attack as a sign of the British hand in the operation. Then, weeks later on July 15, there was an attempted coup d'etat to remove Erdogan as president. Putin was one of the first and one of the few world leaders to call Erdogan to offer support for the stability of the Turkish nation.

In this context, in their meeting on Aug. 9, Putin and Erdogan discussed re-establishing economic relations, emphasizing the Turkish Stream natural gas pipeline and Russian nuclear power technology. In addition to such economic collaboration, they also made a commitment to deal with the Syrian crisis, establishing a joint task force involving top officials of the military, intelligence services, and foreign ministries. Erdogan identified the key role of Russia in establishing peace in Syria, and called for mutual action by Russia and Turkey—and with Iran. He also pointed to the fallacy of distinguishing "good" from "bad" terrorists, calling it an "incorrect approach." Obama and his British Imperial handlers have played this game *ad nauseam* for their geopolitical aims.

The profound nature of Putin's intervention was further elaborated the day before in Baku, Azerbaijan, when he met with Iranian President Hassan Rouhani and Azerbaijan's President Ilham Aliyev for discussions on the International North-South Transport Corridor—the 4,500-mile corridor running from the Arabian Sea to Scandinavia. They also considered a draft declaration for joint work against terrorism. The North-South Transport Corridor project will now engage Russia, Azerbaijan, Turkey, and Iran, and will fold into China's "One Belt, One Road" project of the New Silk Road. The Russia-Turkey partnership will bring greater

Turkish citizens in Istanbul on July 19, 2016, demonstrating against the coup attempt.

stability to the entire Caspian Sea, Caucasus, and Balkan region, extending the zone of Eurasian security and prosperity further west.

Concerning the meetings between Putin and Erdogan, and the previous day's meeting in Azerbaijan, Lyndon LaRouche said that "the course of history has been changed" by the agreements reached, and the agreements that will follow from the Putin-Erdogan summit. Turkey can play a pivotal role in that North-South Transport Corridor and the Putin-Erdogan meeting will serve to advance that deeper collaboration.

LaRouche continued, "What I saw as a possibility has now been realized. A new alignment of Eurasia is now moving forward, and whatever efforts Obama and NATO might make to stop it are now too little, too late."

These developments have put the British Imperial policy of the "Great Game" in jeopardy, such that it will be increasingly difficult to manipulate the Turkic populations of Central Asia into hosting terrorist activities against Russia, China, and India.

Know Thine Enemy

The North-South Transport Corridor is a critical element of the New Silk Road, or World Land-Bridge concept that Lyndon LaRouche and Helga Zepp-LaRouche have been organizing for more than 25 years. As this concept comes into focus, along with the attendant collaboration in space exploration and the cultural ex-

change that was also a key aspect of the ancient Silk Road, this bundle of associated developments now lays the foundation for a Renaissance that is global in its reach.

Previous Renaissances have been localized, but for the first time in the history of humanity, a global Renaissance is now an active potential. Whether the forces of the British Empire understand this full potential or not is irrelevant. They will seek to crush anything that represents a modicum of optimism for humanity. And given the Empire's current state of desperation in the context of the trans-Atlantic financial meltdown, it is reacting by organizing world war, potentially all the way to the use of thermonuclear weapons.

The British Imperial oligarchs—and their hands and feet in the City of London and Wall Street—reacted the same way when the great projects of the late 19th Century, inspired by the "American System," began to emerge. As the Trans-Siberian Railway and the Berlin-to-Baghdad Railway were being built, the potential to unite Europe to Asia via Russia threatened the very existence of the British Empire and its control of the sea lanes. Halford Mackinder, the godfather of British geopolitics, who inspired and organized the geopolitical doctrine of the Nazis through Karl Haushofer, knew that the key to control was the "divide and rule" strategy of pitting nations and peoples against each other.

Scene of a car bombing in Ankara, Turkey, Feb. 17, 2016.

CC/Yildiz Yazicioglu

Understanding this arc of history is critical to the security policy of the next presidency, because anyone who accepts the present narrative about the nature of terrorism, will either be a witting tool or an unwitting dupe of the British Empire. The use of terrorism in the Middle East and Central Asia is nothing but the extension of this British Imperial "Great Game" concept of the middle of the 19th Century. The terrorists of ISIS and Al-Qaeda today were spawned from the terrorists in Chechnya of the late 1990s, who in turn were spawned by Osama Bin Laden's Mujahedeen in Afghanistan in the 1980s—all in the same role as mercenaries deployed by the British Empire for warfare against the leading nations of Eurasia, below the nuclear threshold.

This use of terrorism for geopolitical aims was recently exposed by the declassification of the "28 Pages" in the United States and the issuing of the *Chilcot Report* in the United Kingdom, both released in the same week in early July.

The 28 Pages point to the role of the Kingdom of Saudi Arabia in organizing the terrorist attacks on our nation on September 11, 2001. The Bush Administration's classification of the 28 Pages—the final chapter of the Joint Congressional Inquiry into 9/11—was essential to the build-up to war against Iraq based on lies—the same lies which are at the center of the Chilcot Report, which showed Tony Blair's critical role in organizing a war of aggression against Iraq, on behalf of Her Majesty the Queen. The recent interview on 28pages.org with Larry Wilkerson, former chief of staff for Colin Powell, revealed once more how Dick Cheney personally suppressed the truth about the Saudi role in 9/11, in order to push the lie that Saddam Hussein was behind the terrorist attack on the United States. That lie was used to manipulate the United Nations, and the world, into supporting a war against Iraq.

However, as blatant as these lies and deceptions may be, Lyndon LaRouche has always pointed to the "Al-Yamamah" deal as central to the whole operation of 9/11 and the ensuing global war policy. Under the Al-Yamamah deal, British Aerospace, now called BAE Systems, provided military hardware and fighter jets to the Kingdom of Saudi Arabia over the recent decades, in exchange for one tanker of oil per day for the duration of the deal. Using the profit of oil sold over and above the cost of the arms, the British created a slush fund of tens of billions of dollars, if not hundreds of billions, that has financed terrorism ever since, for geopolitical aims.

One of the central figures in the 28 Pages, who provided logistical support to the terrorist network behind 9/11, Prince Bandar Bin Sultan, was the key organizer of the Al-Yamamah deal while he was the Saudi Ambassador to the United States from 1983 to 2005. At that time, the United States was supporting Osama Bin Laden and the Mujahedeen for the purposes of geopolitical control. In a 2014 interview with Charlie Rose, Prince Bandar spoke of his meeting with Osama Bin Laden, who expressed gratitude for his support of the Mujahedeen. Bandar said, "He came to thank me for my efforts to bring the Americans, our friends, to help us against the atheists, he said, the Communists."

Those responsible for 9/11 and the ensuing lies to launch wars of aggression that have destroyed global security, must be brought to justice. The truth of terrorism must now be told, and anyone who dismisses it as simply "conspiracy theory" is either working for the enemy, or has been behavior-modified. Telling the truth is essential to building an international coalition against terrorism, working with the nations who are ultimately the main targets—Russia, China, and India. However, simply killing terrorists will not solve the problem on its own. We need global economic development as the true path to peace, based on the principle of "the advantage of the other."

Security and the Four Laws

"Only principles of intention which have a constitutional basis in natural law, rather than positive law, such as the great constitutional principle, 'the advantage of the other,' of the 1648 Treaty of Westphalia, could succeed in establishing a core-agreement in circumstances such as those of this region today. The positive law must wait upon the pleasure of the adoption of the relevant, ecumenical principles of natural law."

—The LaRouche Doctrine for Southwest Asia
(*EIR*, April 17, 2004)

painting by Gerard Terborch

The signing of the Peace of Westphalia (Münster), 1648.

The Treaty of Westphalia ended the Thirty Years War, which had ravaged Europe with religious warfare until that treaty was signed in 1648. The treaty explicitly stated that the end of the warfare must be based on mutual cooperation. The 21st Century version of this principle is at the economic, scientific, and diplomatic frontier of the unprecedented new paradigm now unfolding on the Eurasian landmass. The leadership of China has referred to this principle of mutual benefit in its One Belt, One Road program as "win-win."

Historic points of tension and conflict that have been manipulated by British Imperial geopolitics, such as those between Russia and China, India and Pakistan, Russia and Turkey, and China and Japan, are now being resolved by the same principled approach that ended the Thirty Years War. It was none other than Tony Blair who called for the end of the Westphalian Era in a 1999 speech in Chicago, where he launched the concept of "Responsibility to Protect" (R2P), which has been used by the Chicago-based Obama murder machine to launch wars of imperial rampage, such as Libya and Syria.

It was Lyndon LaRouche and Helga Zepp-LaRouche who established the dialogue and the policy initiative that have led to the One Belt, One Road program and myriad associated and derivative projects, such as the North-South Transport Corridor. What is critical now, is that forces within the trans-Atlantic region, especially within the institution of the Presidency of the United States, engage with the LaRouches in that dialogue immediately.

LaRouche's "Four Laws" provide the guiding principles for an economic recovery that is crucial for ending the U.S. policy of imperial rampaging, directed by the British Monarchy. In 2014, Helga Zepp-LaRouche called for a "New Security Architecture," writing that "we immediately need a global emergency conference with only a single theme: How should a global, inclusive security architecture be designed which guarantees the existence and security of all nations on the planet?"

Central to this New Security Architecture will be the acceptance of Vladimir Putin's offer made at last year's UN General Assembly, for an international coalition against terrorism, and acceptance of President Xi Jinping's offer, made at the APEC Summit in 2014, to join the global development program around the New Silk Road concept. Let us resolve to bring the world together based on the principle of "the advantage of the other," and to end this dark age of warfare by launching a new Renaissance for humanity.

On the 'Four Laws' And *The Hamiltonian*

The following comments are excerpted and edited from the LaRouche PAC Webcast of Aug. 12, 2016.

Host Matthew Ogden: Michael, maybe you can say a bit about the subject of *The Hamiltonian* broadsheet just released in Manhattan by the LaRouche movement.

Michael Steger: Sure! I think it's worth stating in terms of the international picture, that over these last 15 years since the 9/11 attacks, every major political institution, whether it be a political party, a branch of government, or a grass-roots organization, has largely been discredited by the inability to either stand up to the Bush and Obama regimes, or to not be bought out and compromised by them,— except for what our organization has largely done.

That creates a real political vacuum in the United States. As we've seen with both of these candidates, they're despised by a majority in their parties, and an increasing majority of the American people. And so when you look at the New Presidency, the way Lyn's laid it out—he laid this out, this paper, "The Four New Laws to Save the United States Now," —this was two years ago.

The perspective was clear from Lyn's vantage point, that we're at a point where there is no institution in the United States—political body, think tank—that has any clue at all of how to deal with the current unfolding crisis. On one side, there's the immediate war danger, and the political breakdown of the European Union, NATO, trans-Atlantic system. At the same time, there's the breakdown of the financial system. But they're not separate. They are the same fundamental system that is now facing a kind of moral bankruptcy, a collapse of

> The perspective was clear … that we're at a point where there is no institution in the United States—political body, think tank—that has any clue at all of how to deal with the currently unfolding crisis.

any real value to human society.

Clearly, nations like Germany, Italy, and the United States have a real role to play in the overall development perspectives. But you have to see things in the context of this breakdown. What Lyn put forward,— we've seen it,— we've seen the resurgence of Glass-Steagall. Both parties' platforms now have it. There's a clear recognition, broadly, among the American people, of what would seem to be an arcane banking-regulation policy. But, as many people have grown to recognize, it's really the major tool to dismantle this Wall Street apparatus, this kind of criminal financial fraud that's been perpetrated, recklessly, without any real control, for the last 15 years, and really much longer.

The New Presidency

The question that Lyn raised, was what is a competent government at this point, especially in the United States— a real, competent form of policy? And there has to be a commitment toward the future of mankind, long term. He said this repeatedly in the recent period. We cannot base these steps we're going to take, on the past. We have to base *our* solution on the future. What Russia, under Putin, and China are now doing, is consolidating a very bright future for the majority of mankind, with the collaboration of nations which have huge geo-strategic past problems, but recognize now the economic question of collaboration between China and India, India, and Pakistan, Iran with other nations in the Caucusus, and with Russia.

This kind of collaboration and integration of Eurasia is really a remarkable question. And in that, you have a driving policy led by China regarding space exploration and fusion research. China is one of the world leaders today in fusion research capabilities, as is South Korea. You have a capability there for the United States to orient to, around the Four Laws, which is, first, Glass-Steagall. The second is a National Banking system. That means you have a banking system which now has the capability, regulated by the office of the Treasury, of a kind of Greenback-like Lincoln policy. The Third Law is that we define what a federal credit system is for. It's not just a federal credit system. You don't just allow the federal government now to just print credit. *We define it from a physical-economic standpoint of the future,* what is necessary for mankind's long-term survival. And that's where the collaboration of nations like Russia, China, and India becomes so essential, because these questions of space exploration and fusion power really define that. And that really is the Fourth Law, which is a collaboration with these nations, around this kind of scientific advancement of mankind.

Our perspective, which I think what should be an increasing perspective of the American people, who tend to find themselves distraught by this Presidential election,— is not to cower in fear, or hide somewhere in a hole, waiting for it to all end, but to recognize that there's a political vacuum, where our leadership is essential, and that these policies are the immediate steps that any President has to take. If not, we're not going to regain or reconstitute a Constitutional American Presidency. But the Four Laws are actually going to secure the physical livelihood of the United States for the generations to come, and that really is the intervention that has to be made on the new Presidency. There will be a series of articles. Kesha Rogers' second article was released in *EIR* magazine yesterday, and there will be a follow-up article next week by Dave Christie (see p. 7, this issue), and there will be more to come.

Ogden: Well, absolutely filling that political vacuum is

> **…the Four Laws are actually going to secure the physical livelihood of the United States for the generations to come, and that really is the intervention that has to be made on the new Presidency…**

what *The Hamiltonian* is serving to do. I think it's already having a radiating effect. Diane, if you want to just jump in and discuss a little bit of the effect in New York.

Diane Sare: Well, first I'll just start by saying that Manhattan is the political center of the United States; and it's certainly the political center of these two campaigns. Both Hillary Clinton and Donald Trump are based in this area. And I will also say the population is clearly anguished. We talked last week about how Hillary's campaign is providing cover for Obama to run his war and provocation policy. And I think the weakness that we're filling in, is that Americans have been so bereft of a future, or of thinking of a future, that they're not able to think strategically. So, many people have questions about, "Why is Putin working with Erdogan; isn't Erdogan horrible? Didn't he do these horrible things?" Well, he did do horrible things, but there is a strategic shift where it's become very clear that the interest of Turkey is tied up in the new BRICS dynamic, that a *New Paradigm* has been created, and in a sense, that's what we are creating here.

The Spirit of Man

I actually was sent something from one of our collaborators on the West Coast, which I think is really

en.wikipedia.org
Hillary Rodham Clinton at the London meeting to discuss NATO military intervention in Libya, 29 March 2011.

Wikimedia Commons/Michael Vadon
Donald Trump, Jr.

delightful in terms of an approach to how to think properly. It's comments from Helen Keller when she got an opportunity to go up in the Empire State Building and "look" out at Manhattan. I think everyone knows—hopefully—that Helen Keller was both blind and deaf; but her insights into these matters are the more striking and more profound. In fact, she speculates that she and her friend who was blind, had a much better view of Manhattan from the top of the Empire State Building than the people who had two good eyes. Her description is somewhat delightful. She says that "It was a thrilling experience to be whizzed in a lift a quarter of a mile heavenward, and to see New York spread out like a marvelous tapestry beneath us. There was the Hudson, more like the flash of a sword blade than a noble river. The little island of Manhattan, set like a jewel in its nest of rainbow waters, stared up into my face. And the Solar system circled about my head. Why, I thought, the Sun and the stars are suburbs of New York and I never knew it." I think that makes her a New Yorker for sure.

She said, "I have this sort of wild desire to invest in a bit of real estate on one of the planets. All sense of depression and hard times vanished. I felt like being frivolous with the stars."

Then, she talks about the construction of the Empire State Building as itself being poetical. She says, "From everyone except my blind friend, I had received an impression of sordid materialism. The piling up of one steel honeycomb upon another with no real purpose but to satisfy the American craving for the superlative in everything. Well, I see in the Empire Building something else—passionate skill, arduous and fearless idealism. The tallest building is a victory of imagination. Instead of crouching close to Earth like a beast, the spirit of man soars to higher regions. And from this new point of vantage, he looks upon the impossible with fortified courage, and dreams yet more magnificent enterprises."

This reminds me so much of what President Kennedy about why we go to the Moon; or Krafft Ehricke's sense of the extraterrestrial imperative for mankind. It's our job here—particularly in Manhattan, where I think people may be most susceptible to it; because in Manhattan we are blessed with an extraordinarily diverse population from all over the world. It's not simply that

> **…the idea is to rekindle a spark of a certain quality of American identity which is a love of the future, a love of the potential for what mankind can contribute to the future…**

you have the headquarters of the United Nations. But if you think of what the population is in Queens and Brooklyn and New Jersey, where I am, and the surrounding areas,— the Statue of Liberty and Ellis Island had something to do with this many years ago. You have a population which actually is in touch with the rest of the world. So, there are people in this area that have a sense that the whole world is not going to Hell; that in some places, having a pothole that could swallow up a double-decker bus is actually considered a sign of poverty, and you're supposed to repair it and do something about it—as opposed to what people have begun to take for granted here. So, the idea is to rekindle a spark of a certain quality of American identity which is a love of the future, a love of the potential for what mankind can contribute to the future, which I think Helen Keller expresses so magnificently in that piece.

I would just say—Mike alluded to this—on the question of Sept. 11: one person I spoke with said last night that her uncle had just passed away two days ago. He was someone who had worked there, and suffered from various kinds of lung disease and finally died. The death toll from these attacks has not ended, and it's not only the people in New York who were first responders. It's people who were killed in these wars which I think we're going to take up a bit more, these wars that were totally unjustified, that were based on lies and cover-ups from the Bush Administration through the Obama Administration.

If we can address that, at this fifteenth anniversary, that we end this period of injustice and of criminal wars of aggression,— I think you could see a real shift. It's as if the American people have had a heavy manhole cover on top of their brains and on top of their identities, and they haven't even allowed themselves to think of what the potential is. In those circumstances, I think all bets are off, even in terms of this ridiculous scenario that we're calling a Presidential election. There's nothing to say that these two mentally unstable characters passing for Presidential candidates, have to be the candidates by the time we get to November. So, it's a very, very rich moment, and it's just urgent that everybody who hears what we are saying and what the LaRouche Movement is doing, who gets our literature, moves to circulate it and mobilize as many people as you can.

A View from Inside LaRouche's Manhattan Project

by Daniel Burke

Aug. 16—Every Saturday afternoon around 12:30 PM, I cross the George Washington Bridge in my car, on my way to a meeting in Manhattan with Lyndon LaRouche. Habitually, I turn my gaze south, along the length of the island. When we arrive at the meeting, LaRouche causes his presence to appear on a large screen in front of a group of people, each of whom has made his or her own trip, whether short or long. Over the course of ninety minutes or so, a sequence of people take their places in front of a microphone to engage in a dialogue with LaRouche. More often than not, I find myself in that line of people, with a question or report. He responds to me, as he does to each person who addresses him. But he does so in an unusual way.

What I find is that LaRouche has a respect for the human mind, one that is greater than my own, but to which I aspire. If I stand before a crowd of our political activists, a group of courageous people who dare face the true threat of thermonuclear war, and present an undiscriminating or false view, as I have more than once, he provides me with a means of correction. Not by suggesting better opinions than my own, but by compelling me to devote myself to something better than mere opinion.

He expressed that idea in our last Saturday dialogue in the following way:

Society requires leadership, which is not leadership in any bullying way. It's a question of saying, "What is the purpose of my life, since I know it's not going to continue?" And therefore, you devote yourself to trying to create, in and of yourself, something which you think has a higher mortality rate, that is a good mortality rate.... The devotion to the mission, not just *a* mission, but the mission of the future of development of mankind, without regard to mere life mortality.

Those of us who choose to see it will acknowledge now, that should the United States fail to be guided by this quality of leadership, the human species may be extinguished.

Each hour of every day of August 2016, the American people are subjected to an ever-uglier cacophony of opinions. As you walk down the street, you hear the snippets of conversation from citizens bewildered and dismayed.

"We can't have Hillary — she's a liar, and she'll just make more war."

"Yes, but the other guy's a racist pig!"

"Well anyway, you have to choose one!"

EIRNS/Dana Carsrud

LaRouche PAC rally at UN Headquarters, Sept. 28, 2015.

The people are repulsed by the failure of their own opinions, and the undeniably Satanic quality of their leadership. There is something that doesn't work about the approach that society at large has accepted: to tolerate a life as a slave to popular opinion. The standards used to train our children will not cause them to become geniuses, and we need geniuses. The standards of "repeat after teacher" will not create a future amidst the collapse of economic, political, and cultural life.

Dedication

I have seen that recognition, an awareness of one's own desire for true substance, flash across the faces of many New Yorkers, as a LaRouche activist calls to them in the street, "Get a copy of LaRouche's new paper, *The Hamiltonian!*" Many recognize LaRouche as an historic personality, but many do not. The look of concern on their brows as they examine the headline is enough for me to know that they have some taste of the matter at hand: that they might have to learn how the world really works, this week, lest they wake up to find that the meaning of their life has been taken from them.

By the end of this week, ten thousand copies of *The Hamiltonian,* "The Voice of the LaRouche Political Movement," will have made their way into the hands of New Yorkers. As the British-aligned forces of Obama and Hillary escalate evil war propaganda against Russia, in particular, and China, we have devoted ourselves to creating a network of activists capable of distributing this broadsheet at strategic locations all around the city—Lower Manhattan, where we continue to meet 9/11 survivors passionate about the need for justice; the Upper West Side, territory of Obama and Hillary that we're now reclaiming for Hamilton; Midtown, beneath the towers of Soros and the condominiums owned by Saudi Royals; even in the subway station beneath the New York Times building.

Our activists, recruited by LaRouche directly at our Saturday meetings, increasingly recognize the responsibility we hold, to educate the nation and the institution of the Presidency on what principles will rescue the U.S. economy. As the institutions of the trans-Atlantic system crumble, and the New Paradigm of Russia and China and the BRICS as a whole marches towards a "win-win" future, we have the task of bringing the United States into that new world economic order.

With our eyes set on the principles of a real human, Hamiltonian economy, which principles are the basis for Lyndon LaRouche's accurate strategic forecasts over more than fifty years, activists within the Manhattan Project see processes clearly that are hidden from most people. But to reveal to ourselves and our fellow citizens what those processes mean for each of us individually,— this depends on the aspect of the Manhattan Project that serves no purpose exterior to itself—the music.

In discussion with his Policy Committee Monday, Aug. 15, LaRouche presented it in the following way:

> Take the music work we're doing now. What're we doing that for?! We're doing that to create something, what? What're we trying to create? We're trying to create something greater than was ever created before. And you use music, for example, composition as a medium for that purpose. That's what drives you. That keeps you free from shame.

At this point, the Schiller Institute of Lyndon and Helga LaRouche has initiated four separate choruses in the New York area, with plans for a fifth. Each of these choruses has participated in broad outreach into the city, recruiting new members, singing before new audiences, learning new works. Over the weekend of the fifteenth anniversary of the 9/11 attacks, *in memoriam* of the victims of those attacks and of their aftermath, members of these choruses will come together to sing Mozart's *Requiem,* several African-American spirituals, and other classical works, in a series of concerts hosted by the New York-based Foundation for the Revival of Classical Culture.

I am not a highly trained musician, nor am I a deeply knowledgeable student of music. But the curious thing I can state with certainty is that the conductor of a classical chorus has a relationship to each individual singer that is very similar to the relationship LaRouche has to the participants and audience of his Saturday dialogues. I am convinced that musical beauty is not a matter of having the right opinion or interpretation. To place the voice properly is a matter of one's dedication to a truth conveyed socially, one which allows others to find in themselves a reflection of their own true mind. So let us dedicate ourselves to a form of leadership that is not dependent on seeking an advantage over the opinions of others. Compel our citizens to develop a strength of mind, by first becoming aware of it.

How We Defeat Evil

Excerpts of Lyndon LaRouche in Dialogue with the Manhattan Project, Saturday, Aug. 13, 2016.

Dennis Speed: On behalf of the LaRouche Political Action Committee, I'd like to welcome everybody here today, for our Aug. 13 dialogue with Lyndon LaRouche. I think most of you here have received a copy of the broadsheet *The Hamiltonian,* and we're fully in business now as a very active force in Manhattan.

Lyn, I'd like for you to give us some opening remarks, and then we'll go right into questions and answers.

Lyndon LaRouche: Well, we're in a situation now where everything that's wrong in the United States has to be corrected. It's that simple. But now we find that there are certain numbers among the members of this organization, who are working on trying to solve these problems. What I can do is not to solve these problems as such, but perhaps to guide some of our members here and elsewhere to get a better grip on what they can do to change the situation in the United States and beyond.

Bill Roberts: Hi, Lyn. I've been asked to try to describe a process which is underway now, as the Manhattan choral process expands into the outer boroughs with the process of organizing for the series of concerts that are taking place, the "Living Memorial for 9/11."

Statue of Alexander Hamilton in front of the U.S. Treasury Building. Sculptor: James Earl Fraser (1878-1953).

EIRNS/Stuart Lewis

This is intersecting—you could call it an ecumenical process is taking place. I think it's a reflection of the way in which the Westphalian principle throughout the world is finding its way into New York, really, and intersecting this process of the Manhattan choral principle expanding outward. I can just give a few examples. We were in an Irish neighborhood in the Bronx, telling people that we had been the ones who had organized the concert commemorating the 50th anniversary of the Kennedy family's concert held in honor of John F. Kennedy, to which the Irish President sent a message, and it's with that same spirit that we are organizing this concert in the Bronx. We were in the Italian neighborhood, and a shoe salesman—a shop owner whose children have been trained in Classical music—wants us to start a community chorus and wants us to use the church in the neighborhood in the Bronx.

We also had a meeting with the board of a certain mosque, and this was interesting because it was in the aftermath of this priest being killed in France. There was a deliberate decision that was made by the Pope that the service that was going to be held to honor this priest, was going to include a large number of Muslims. There was very explicitly this Abraham Lincoln sort of idea of "with malice towards none." These are people who immediately respond to the idea of what we are doing with the "Living Memorial to 9/11" in honor of all the victims of those attacks and their aftermath, and the process of wars and terrorism that have come as a process of the cover-up of how that was organized. So, they would like to help us.

Several weeks ago, just as another example of this, for the first time at a Puerto Rican cultural center, instead of the usual sort of music that they put on, we had a Classical musical concert in this Latino center. So, maybe you just want to comment, because there's a sort of process now underway which is a little bit hard to describe, but it is intersecting these different communities, who see the intervention that we're making as very important for their communities and for their young people.

No Answer Without Hamilton

LaRouche: Well, I don't want to distract from those concerns; but if you want to get at the core of the United States and its effective leadership, you have to go back to Alexander Hamilton. Now, there are a lot of people who would follow Alexander Hamilton in certain suggestions; but they do not understand the effect and importance of Alexander Hamilton's expression. Without Alexander Hamilton's tradition, you could not have a solution for any of these problems. That's the thing you've got to look at. And you've got to look at what it's going to take, to bring forth in the United States from them and their souls as such, to understand what Alexander Hamilton represents for the history of the United States and of the world.

Question: Hello, Mr. LaRouche. My question is toward 9/11 and the victims from the attack and the aftermath. I had an uncle who was not there that day, but he worked for the building and he was part of the cleanup, and he just passed recently. I'm reading more and more about people that are still dying. I just lost an uncle, and I'm reading more and more victims are still dying to this day. Even though the reports from the "28 Pages" are just starting to surface, we're not getting justice, we're not coming to the light of what really happened. We're trying to strive for the truth of it, we're trying to bring justice, but the criminals who did that terrible act that day and put it into action, what can we do more to bring justice...?

LaRouche: Yes; the first thing you've got to do is go back; and you've got to go back to Alexander Ham-

ilton. Again, the Hamilton tradition of the United States is the key to the survival of the United States; without that, you don't get a survival.

Now, what's the issue here? The issue is that essentially Obama is an enemy of what was represented by Alexander Hamilton, in spades. Therefore, you've got to look for solutions and not for symbols. In other words, a symbolic gesture is not a success intrinsically. So you've got to look at where's the generation of this.

Now, I've observed actively in a photographic process of what went on in 9/11. I went through every page of 9/11 as it was being presented, as the people who were being thrown out of the buildings from which they were burned. So therefore, the question is, how do you solve that problem? And what's the answer? The answer is, again, Alexander Hamilton. The problem inclusively is the members of the Congress who have allowed the alleged legitimacy of the practices of the members of the Congress and of other people who shared those opinions.

Without getting at the combination of Alexander Hamilton's role and his personal sacrifice, to create and develop this nation, you would not have had a U.S. nation. It wouldn't have happened. And everything that has hit us—and I've also gone through this—I watched what was happening with the towers; it was photographic, but it was active. I saw what happened, step by step. From Boston to Washington, and to the present premises. So, you've got to go to attack the problem by the name of the cause of the problem, and how you can bring a solution to that problem, by identifying precisely what has to be stopped,—I'm saying,—should have been stopped.

Question: Hello, Mr. LaRouche; it's Howard from New York. We've been able to do some campaigning this week, we've been getting these out—*The Hamiltonian* newspaper—in Manhattan on the role of Hillary Clinton as a stooge of Obama and the war drive. We're still thinking in the back of our head that we are having an election for President; somebody of some sort has to become the President of the United States in January 2017. What are we supposed to think when we hear the rather poor campaign, the rather defective campaign of Donald Trump, say that Hillary Clinton and Barack Obama founded ISIS, the terrorist organization? Is there something real here, with him saying this, or is this just whatever?

kremlin.ru

Russian President Vladimir Putin (right) with Kyrgyzstan President Almazbek Atambayev at the Supreme Eurasian Economic Council meeting in expanded format.

Putin's Influence

LaRouche: This is the problem of the citizens of the United States, who have not agreed to do what they should have done. That's the problem. The cowardice of the citizens of the United States is the problem. Now, what is the cause of the problem? How does the problem work? The way the problem works is that popular opinion, or a certain section of popular opinion, is now saying you have to respect, you have to give them a chance, you have to give them an option, you have to give them an explanation. All this has been done; and it did no damned good at all. It's still not good enough.

The Hamilton principle is the recipe; and get that Hamilton principle in mind. Look at Hamilton's mind from inside his mind. Look at it from the beginning of his rise to power and influence in Philadelphia, and what he did in the whole process of developing the United States. This man, Alexander Hamilton, is the hard core of the continued existence of the United States. If you don't get at that issue, you're going to fail because you haven't got a weapon which is effective enough to do the job you want to do.

Question: Just one follow-up. I know that the Russians have been very vocal about this, but do you have anything to add on to what we can do about the phenomenon ongoing of ISIS and international terrorism?

LaRouche: I can tell you what's going on. It's

largely Putin. Putin has built up a very respectable organization which now occupies much of our entire planet! He has pulled together groups of nations which are the most respected, in general, and the most efficient, and the ones which are most likely to cure the problem. That's what the problem is. It's when people say, "Well, yes, but,—yes, but,—yes, but." "You can't talk about our President right now," because what is our President? Our President is a substitute for Satan. What do you want? You got him! Some of these people are trying to get him in there again, and you find that most of the people in the Congress are corrupt—terribly corrupt. The leading candidates are terribly corrupt. So you're going to worry about which candidate you're going to elect? When you know that all the candidates, chiefly,— that you're talking about are specimens of evil? That in one way or the other, they reject their responsibilities as human beings for this process.

So, we've got to get at the *source* of the problem, not trying to find a solution for the problem. Find the source of the problem, and bring about a removal of the source of the problem.

Question: Lyn, this week we had this major turnaround between Putin and Erdogan of Turkey, where they met; and I'm thinking about Hamilton in terms of the reflection that we see in Putin's personality and his action. Because we very nearly had a World War III last year, on the basis of the Turkish action on behalf of Obama, to shoot down the Russian airplane. And yet, here we are, less than a year later actually, and in resolving this crisis, Putin has made agreements on the Turkish Stream Pipeline, such that Turkey is going to pay half of it and I believe Russia is going to pay the other half. In addition, new nuclear power plants being planned in Turkey. And even the cooperation in Syria is on the agenda in a very serious way.

It reminds me of the Hamiltonian idea of the Erie Canal; that you have to actually change the strategic situation, the context of strategy, if you're going to win a victory over empire. That was a method that we saw demonstrated this week by Putin, which was exciting, inspiring, surprising. So, I wonder if you can comment on that?

LaRouche and Putin

LaRouche: I was not at all surprised about what happened the past week; I knew it was coming. I affirmed the fact that I knew it was coming. What did he do? What did he incorporate? Putin's influence is not only Russia: other parts of the whole Asiatic area are loaded with it. Putin is already the working President of a new universe. He hasn't gotten any other people to do the job for him, but he's the one figure who is doing the best job right now.

What's wrong with us, that we believe in ideas which are stupid? Supporters of Hillary Clinton at the Democratic Convention.

What you have is, you have a bunch of people in the United States who ruined themselves and ruined the nation by condoning things that they shouldn't condone, things that they are actually promoting as destruction. What we need to do is get Obama thrown out, out of his office. Get similar types of creeps out. Push them out fast! Get together people who will sum up to an affirmation of the memory of our great leader, Alexander Hamilton. That's the way to do it; go for victory.

Now, he was killed by a British agent, and people in the system condoned his assassination. And that's a fact we should remember. Let me just add one thing here. Putin was, as a child, from a family of Russians who were fighting the Nazis as such. He, in the course of his life, developed a very strong and efficient understanding of what has to be done to protect humanity against evil; evil like Chechens, for example. The Chechens are your typical evil ones of this time. So, what he did— and I followed him; I didn't actually meet him personally, but I followed him in great detail during major parts of his career. I understood what he was doing, and I understood the effect of what he was doing. So, you're getting an Alexander Hamilton similarity for Russia— not only Russia, but for Asia! For *all of Asia,* practically. That's a pretty big item.

Therefore, what we have to do is understand, what's wrong with us, that we believe in the kinds of ideas which we condone in us, ideas which are stupid? That's where the problem lies. We have to get the act of our people cleaned up. Don't go around and say [whining], "Well, that's not too bad." It stinks buddy, and let's get rid of it!

Joseph Stahleicher: Hello, Lyn. Greetings from Manhattan!

I gladly received *The Hamiltonian,* and my question is, as a continuation of the debate that we have here about Putin: What is the aspect of Bismarck in this connection, because it reminds me a lot of the work Bismarck did in Europe to create a situation of a long duration of peace between East and West and every country in Europe. The question is how we can enforce this debate? In Germany, for instance, we have Steinmeier, we have other people who want to work with Russia. How can we put this Bismarck emphasis into this debate?

LaRouche: What's needed is collaboration, not dictation, and not imposition of any kind. But what you have to do is examine what Putin has been doing.

Now, I have a certain substantial experience with Putin. The funny thing is that I never really spoke to him directly. But I was in the same battle that he was in, from a different card, all through most of his career, either passively or actively,— but always very actively, because I knew what he is. I understood him. I don't know everything about him. I haven't talked to him, obviously, directly, but I do know what his history is, how he dealt with the Chechens for example.

And now, what he's done, in his history, is that he has recognized the way to deal with the way in which the Nazis *en masse* killed many of his family, and many Russians as well. And so therefore, it's not vengeance as such, or things like that. It's the fact that we all have to do as I did in my support of Putin; that is, I was not one of his workers, I was not one of his representatives, but I was one of his leading supporters in a certain moment of his history. And so what people should have to do, is do the things that are the good things, which make the good manifest among the people.

And wherever you go along in life, wherever you have a chance to do good, do good.

Question: My question is this: I want to know why I haven't heard anything here about supporting the only person that has come out of the political shadows, out of no place, and has been brave enough to stand up and fight, and speak against this, and has put his family and himself at risk to come against the new world order and to come out and run for President of the United States. I support everything that's happening here, but I'd like to understand why there isn't complete support for Donald Trump for President of the United States? That's my question.

LaRouche and Bill Clinton

LaRouche: Okay, well, let's clean this thing up a little bit. I know answers which were not the answers that you were looking for, but which would be useful in illustrating for you, what the problem is that I have to deal with on this thing.

Now, the thing that was significant was my relationship with Bill Clinton. I was allowed to get out of prison, in which I'd been put by the Bush family,— and it was a crime all the way through: a lie and a crime! And the Bushes and so forth were always liars. There has not been a good Bush, anywhere. You try to burn the Bushes and they don't burn, they just stink.

But in any case, what happened is that Putin had, actually, a remote connection to Bill Clinton. And Bill had actually fought a legitimate campaign for leading issues on every leading issue of leading importance, while he was President up to a certain point. But, he also acted as a practical President. He had a very bad Vice President.

He was framed up, and a sex charge was put against him. What had happened is that he had moved to prevent a crisis in German policy and Russia policy as

What did we get? Hillary Clinton became an agent of Obama, and Obama was actually the leading figure of Satan around the world.

well, that would have saved the situation at that time. What happened was, the Queen of England, and by name her leading representatives, and the head of the Republican organization in the United States, all pulled off a frame-up of Bill Clinton. As a result of that, Bill Clinton was stunned and labeled as he was, and it was the Republican Party, largely, that did it, but it was the Queen of England who did it. It was she and her party who did it.

This was a frame-up. The result of this was a breakdown of the order of government of the United States, because of that. In other words, it was a charge against him. I knew what his character was. I did not always approve of what he was doing, but he was an honest person. He had a cause, to save civilization, and it was destroyed by the Queen of England, on her personal order, and her institutions. And by the Republican Party. And they destroyed him!

So you've got to be careful of these things. Don't try to assume that you know this is right and that is right, and this is wrong and that is wrong. It doesn't work that way. You've got to have a deeper insight into how things work, and the problem is that many citizens of the United States don't know the truth. Why don't they know the truth? Because *they don't know how things work,* and therefore they cannot trace out the consequences of evil.

But what did we get? Yes, we got Bill Clinton thrown out of office. *But!* look what he got. Look what his wife got. What was she? She became an agent of

Obama. And Obama was essentially an agent of one of the most evil persons on the planet. He was actually the leading figure of Satan around the world. That's not a good choice of discussion.

Lynne Speed: Hi, Lyn. One of the things that we've been running into with the organizing generally, and then also some of the organizing that we're doing in connection with this 9/11 Living Memorial is, if you just *mention* the idea of this election, and people are almost universally completely disgusted. And it's across the board, so you have Democrats up in East Harlem who are saying "This is the worst thing I've seen in 47 years, since I've been in the country, since I've been voting." You have conservative Tea Party types that have tried all kinds of organizing in the past through activism and so on, who say, "We can't do it that way; we've got to do something which also approaches this at a higher level, a cultural level, which is the way in which you're going to cause people to begin to think."

And at the same time, people are very, very eager for an alternative,— not another candidate, but actually something that both uplifts them, and gives them the power to organize their fellow citizens around a higher conception.

So this week we went down to one of the venues where we're going to be doing one of the concerts, and it was a very interesting discussion, because this particular area, this church is located in an area where there was a firefighters' battalion, over in Brooklyn. They were the closest people to Ground Zero outside of the Ground Zero itself. So they all rushed over when the call came that the Towers had been hit, and they were all inside the building rescuing people, taking them down the steps for about an hour and half, until the building collapsed. The entire battalion was killed, 42 firefighters. And so every year, there's a special ceremony during which they go to the 9/11 memorial and then they march across the bridge and they march to this church where there's a Mass. And we will be singing the *Requiem* as part of that Mass. Our New York Schiller Institute chorus will be participating in that.

What was interesting about this discussion, is that the people in the meeting from the church really got an idea,— from Lynn Yen, who was there at the meeting, and John Sigerson,— that this was a unique idea of doing this Mozart *Requiem* as part of the Mass, and

also because of the way in which we were doing it, at the proper tuning, and because of the entire context, with this being the fifteenth anniversary of 9/11. They were very inspired. They said, "this is what people need. They need to be uplifted, they need to be made spiritually optimistic about the true nature of humanity."

So I just wanted to give you that report and see if you had any comments.

Where the Evil Came From

LaRouche: Well, this is extremely important. It's a fact, of course, it's an important fact. It's a fact which is full of all kinds of illustrations of the way human life goes on. And we will first have to recognize that we have to fight evil. You have to eliminate evil. And if you don't do that, if you can't do that, or just won't, then you are either bad, or you're a failure. And most people in the United States who have lived in the immediately past centuries, have been failures.

And then people say, "well, I want to be a good guy," but they haven't earned it. They haven't earned the credentials. And the important thing is to recognize what the credentials are, or what they might be, and to spread that which might be, at least, and do that. And that is the only way I know of, in which you can reliably indicate what the policy of life in humanity has to be.

Question: Hi Lyn. We're going to have a series of concerts, they're going to be musical concerts. But the most important thing about them, I think is something that Maestro John Sigerson said in a chorus rehearsal on Saturday night, when he was warming us up, getting us to sing. He said, "Look there's a lot of sound. Don't worry about the sound. We have to tune up the chorus so that we can get across the most important idea, which is *silent*. That's why we're doing the work."

So the reason why we have to get people to all four, or one performance, or two performances, is because, as a counterposition to what they experienced as the *evil* of 9/11, they have to experience the emotion that's going to be attendant with them sitting through the *Requiem,* experiencing the *Requiem*—that's the audience and the singers alike. And you also said what I thought you may have said, but do you have some comment on the fact that this—that Americans have to experience this in the near term if we're going to get a solution?

LaRouche: Well, this is a very simple thing to look at. Where was the evil, where did the evil come from? Well, it came from, members of Congress! It came from the President of the United States, and his associates! They're the ones who did it. They made the agreement. Now, here's what they did. The British Empire, working together with the Saudis, created 9/11 in the United States. And those same people, inside the United States, members of the United States who would support this terror operation and still do,— the time has come *to throw these bums out of the Congress!*—and to punish them for what they've done as crimes! Because as long as you have not done that, to clean that thing up, you have no warrant for authority on morality.

Now, I've done that. I've done it to the degree I've been enabled to do that. I was one of the first to expose what was done in the United States, by Great Britain and Saudi Arabia. I was one of the people to expose it—I and an associate of mine, who did it, we were doing it. We were still on the register, of the leading people for exposing what the Satanic operation has been! Obama is himself Satanic! Everything about him: If you look at his history and know what the heritage is, you know he's Satanic. Everything about him is Satanic.

This is not a charge, this is not an accusation. This is an identification! And when you look at it that way, then you know what went wrong. We let the Congress lie.

Now, that's a terrible government, to have a government which lies, where the majority lies. And that's what happened: The Bushes, the Bush family, Obama, they're all in it. And yet, you say you're a citizen of the United States, you are supporting this, and you want to say that you're doing something good? Hey, buddy, you're way off!

The Einstein Question

Speed: Lyn, I have to ask you a question on behalf of Alvin, who is not here. Here's his question: Last week when I talked with you at the meeting here, I informed you of our actions around the "28 pages" petition, the Institute's musical intervention into Spanish Harlem, and then I said, what was missing from our good deeds?

You again raised the example of Einstein, as the model for the kind of quality of mind we are required to develop, if we are to actually move our people into action beyond "good efforts," or "good deeds." Could you please elaborate this further? I still have a long way to go to understand this. It is a difficult concept to grasp fully.

LaRouche: Okay. The Einstein question. The problem is that there's only a tiny, tiny, tiny part of the citizens of the United States in particular, which has any understanding of Einstein, including people running around describing themselves as prophets of Einstein. And this doesn't work either.

You see, the point is, people are saying they're trying to find a prophet, or something like a prophet, in terms of Einstein. Einstein discovered this, Einstein would discovered this… Einstein…. It didn't happen that way!

What had happened was that Einstein, step by step, increasingly understood what was wrong with the way that the people of the world consider how the world works. Now, then the point is, people say, "well the good guys and the bad guys"—buddy, that does not really wash! Because Einstein is not something that you can play with. Einstein was a hero, a great hero of the people of the Universe. Because he dared to make the charges which had to be made, in order to engineer what mankind can do to save the development of the human species. And all these guys who run around saying "this is the recipe for Einstein's this, Einstein's that, Einstein's this"—it's *bunk! Absolute bunk!*

Einstein had a real insight into the *nature* of the Universe, the *nature* of the Universe, *not* the good deeds of somebody else, not the byproducts of good deeds. And there are very few people in this Universe right now, who know what Einstein really was. If you want to argue about it, I'll be pleased to do something about that to help you understand this thing better.

Question: Good afternoon. My name's O— from Staten Island. Last night I was here. You touched on the infancy in terms of one's mindset, and stuff like that—something to that effect. But I just want to know, do you have any books on that?

LaRouche: What, on Einstein?

Question: [follow-up] Yes, on Einstein, and the stuff you're bringing up, or … because this is some fascinating stuff.

LaRouche: No, this is actually science, it's pure science. And what's happened is that there have been people who struggled to understand this sort of thing, and Albert Einstein, in several series of steps of progress, has done the best job, so far, on what the nature of human beings is.

See human beings are not located in the mere *birth* of human beings. What is important is what *goes* with that birth and the development of that birth. And therefore, you often have people who say, "well, this is a good person, this is an expert person, and they're naturally given and this and that, and so forth…" No! No! The question is, can we induce human beings to respond to what Einstein's work really means? Einstein's work was based on the knowledge—I'm not saying the "guess" or this or that—I'm saying "the knowledge" which he has demonstrated and presented, and documented himself. He probably is one of the few people in the Universe right now, who so far has been able to understand what the human mind is. The others are trying to come out and make midgets out of people.

What happens is the person who is creative is *actually creative.* If the individual is not *actually* creative, then he's not actually creative. What do we do? We try to make him *actively* creative—how? By inducing him to understand what he or she can do, to make the human race better, in a necessary way.

But there are all these guys, witch-doctors running around, saying, "this is the way you do this, this is way you inherit, this is the way you inherit…" nonsense! Einstein was very clear on this: You have to look sometimes at his later life works, and they have made that quite clear. And those people who have studied Einstein's work in an advanced way, do understand. I understand.

Speed: What I just was caused to think about, around the Manhattan Project, which you designed—see, you've now said, "Hey, look, guys, you're doing some good things, but it's not ' good deeds.'" And I'd just like to have you say something about your whole method of organizing, which you've been discussing the whole time. Because as we proceed over the next four weeks, we pretty much have all of the pieces now that you've asked us to put together over the course of the year. Now, we're ready—we're ready to go.

So the issue is, being faithful to a method that you've been outlining, to some of us for decades, and to some

cctv

In China's first initiative of its kind, Astronauts on board the Shenzhou-10 spacecraft teach students a lesson through a live video feed system.

of us, for a few months or in a few minutes here. I'd just like you to say something about that.

LaRouche: The whole business of discovery, discovery as such, various degrees of improvement in discovery, progress in discovery, all these things boil down to one thing: That a human being is contributing to the human species, or to the members of the human species, in a way which enables them to have children, to have circumstances of development of children, and so forth. This then extends itself to what Einstein proved. Einstein demonstrated that the Universe is, shall we say, God's Universe. That there's a law, which is a law implicit in Einstein's work, where he understood there was a force in the Universe which was a more powerful force of development of people, as a species. And it's that thing, if you cannot contribute to the development of the species of human beings, especially and most notably— the animal does not have that authority. Only the human being is capable of having that authority, the kind of authority which Albert Einstein had come to understand.

Speed: Thank you very much, Lyn. We're going to move on and do the job you're asking us to do.

LaRouche: Thank you!

III. Lyndon LaRouche: Why Einstein?

LAROUCHE IN DIALOGUE

Einstein's Unique Accomplishment

Lyndon LaRouche in dialogue with the La-Rouche PAC "Basement" Science Team on August 7, 2016, edited.

Lyndon LaRouche: What do you have on your mind?

Benjamin Deniston: You can see Jason and me here; Megan Beets and Liona Fan-Chiang are on via audio, so we've got most of the Basement on.

Jason Ross: Among other topics, it sure seems like we ought to talk about Einstein. You've been talking about him a lot. I recently watched again Shawna's video on Einstein from a couple of years back, and one of the things that she stressed is that Einstein, although a unique individual, also represented something of a culture that existed in Germany at that time, the educational system of Humboldt and Schiller.

LaRouche: There's no difference; Einstein is Einstein and he's one unity which works for all reasons. In other words, he is not a specialist. He's a universalist, that's his character. And what we have not done, we have not probed the implications of Einstein completely enough.

If you look carefully at the recent reports since that time, you see the same thing comes up. The problem is that there are not enough speakers to speak for what Einstein represented. But everything implicitly is there. It is not something you have to poke in there. It was in there originally and it's more so than ever before. But most people don't understand it. Don't blame us, don't blame me; blame them, because they don't know what they're talking about. That's the usual prospect.

Ross: Do you have any advice on foci to start with, to get a sense of this universal character of Einstein? How would you suggest we approach this?

LaRouche: Einstein made his own picture, picture

LPAC TV

Lyndon H. LaRouche, Jr. discussing the Einstein standard for the creative process with members of the LaRouche PAC Policy Committee, a week later on Aug. 15, 2016.

of himself. He did it. He did it repeatedly. But you've got to get into everything he does, everything that he has done in written form or an expressed form. That's what he communicates,— and he's very precise on this matter. He makes discoveries, defines the discoveries, and pushes the discoveries. The problem is, when people are trying to interpret Einstein, that's when they make mistakes. Because they don't understand that the principle of the thing,— there's a principle here as such in Einstein, in what he says, and that's what you get. You want the truth? You get the truth. What's the truth? Einstein understood himself.

Krafft Ehricke

Deniston: One thing we just started to do here, which doesn't address everything he did, is we started in a group, in a social process, reading through his work on relativity, his *Relativity: the Special and General Theory*, that he presented for a general audience.

LaRouche: But the essential thing, is you've got that in the space program, in the foundations of the space program. All of these kinds of things that converge on the same thing, on the Classical space program. You don't have to interpret something; you have to discover what you have seen.

LPAC TV
Members of the LaRouche PAC "Basement" Science Team in an earlier meeting. Left to right: Jason Ross, Liona Fan-Chiang, Benjamin Deniston, and Megan Beets.

Deniston: I wrote something for Kesha Rogers some months back, in which I posed a hypothesis of connecting the space program with the work of Kepler through Einstein, because it's ...

LaRouche: Well, that's fine. That is not only permissible, that is what is demanded.

Deniston: Because it seems to me that what people think about the space program today, is a lot more to do with how do you engineer and implement mankind's ability to get around in space. But before all of that, you had all the actual fundamental discovery of what the Solar system is, and how the Solar system works. And that was really primary, to allow mankind to even have any basis to exist in the Solar system.

LaRouche: The relationships were reciprocal. That is, what you define as the space program, or the principle of the space program, and what you read from the space program, the information, they're mutual. So Einstein, and what Einstein was doing, and the what the founders of the space program were doing, means you have to go back to the space program. What was the space program started on? It started in Germany. That's where it came from, and the space program then was carried through on the basis of that experience, into the program which was done by Krafft Ehricke. And he represented everything to do with it.

Now, and Helga had a thing and I associate myself with it as well, is that on his work, he was in a situation where he was about to die of a disease. He could have lived, if one disease were eliminated, but he couldn't live if he tried to take both of these considerations. And there are people who have been giving pictures on that, who don't know what they're talking about. We have some important names, and on this subject, about Krafft Ehricke, they don't know what they're talking about. And books have been written which were incompetent.

As a matter of fact, the best known records are incompetent, the references to Krafft Ehricke.

You know, Helga also had the same kind of knowledge that I shared with her, with Helga, was the same thing. And our conception was the conception of Krafft Ehricke; that was the real program. The other program of interpretation, accommodated to things, or interpretations, which are contrary to the reality.

Deniston: Well, to me, it seems like this Einstein focus puts it in a different perspective, because it forces the issue more to how does the human mind act to be able to change ...

LaRouche: The same thing. You've got to go back to Germany. You've got to back to the experimental program that was done in a remote area of Germany. And that's the only way can find the truth of the matter.

Deniston: You mean the Peenemünde group?

The Far Side of the Moon

LaRouche: Einstein was part of the same thing. The space program, the space program as originally developed in Germany, is also the root of understanding this part of the matter, and it goes to the question of the nature of man. What is the actual nature of the born man, or the born human being?

All these practical things, all these interpretations, all these books and so forth, are just a mistake. You have to go into the essence of what Einstein was. Because Einstein and the space program are one and the same thing. They are different in terms of theme, but they're equal in terms of motivation.

Look,— what we're waiting for is the China space program, China's space exploration. Because that's something which has fixed value for human knowledge as of now. People get evidence, but the principle is not defined, because the test has not been made. And the test needs to be made in order to solve some of those questions which come up. And as of now, China's work is going to locate it largely in the space program, in getting to the back side of the Moon. What is the back side of the Moon? How does it function? Well, nobody knows. Nobody has yet discovered.

This is a case where an outright space experiment becomes essential. And the same thing with Einstein. Don't try to make a deductive portrait of Einstein, from this program. You have to get in there and prove an experiment, which is what Einstein did. Einstein defined an experiment; all the commentaries about what Einstein's work was, have been wrong, because they didn't do the experiment. Einstein did. And that's the characteristic of his work as a scientist. He perfected the access to nature. But this was based on an experiment, a physical experiment, which was an incomplete perfection; in fact, an imperfect effect is the only thing which is any damned good, right now. The rest of the experiment has not been tested. Everything that Einstein did, has been tested.

Deniston: I don't know how you're thinking about it, but what comes to mind to me, is the question of what's unique about mankind? How is it that mankind can fundamentally change his relation to the universe, in a way no animal species can? For example, moving ...

LaRouche: Mankind is a creator. That is, a creator in the process of becoming a creator. In other words, there's not a difference in this fact, this as opposed to this. But what you get from all good experiment,— which is the kind of experiment that I do, not the kind that most people do, that is the foundation of knowing things. The space program happens to be an experimental program, with all kinds of implications around it, and that is the way you're going to see the unity of what Einstein was doing, on the question of space, and what other people were doing on the question of what happens,— what is space? The problem is that people think they have a grasp of the space program, and they are the ones who make the mistake.

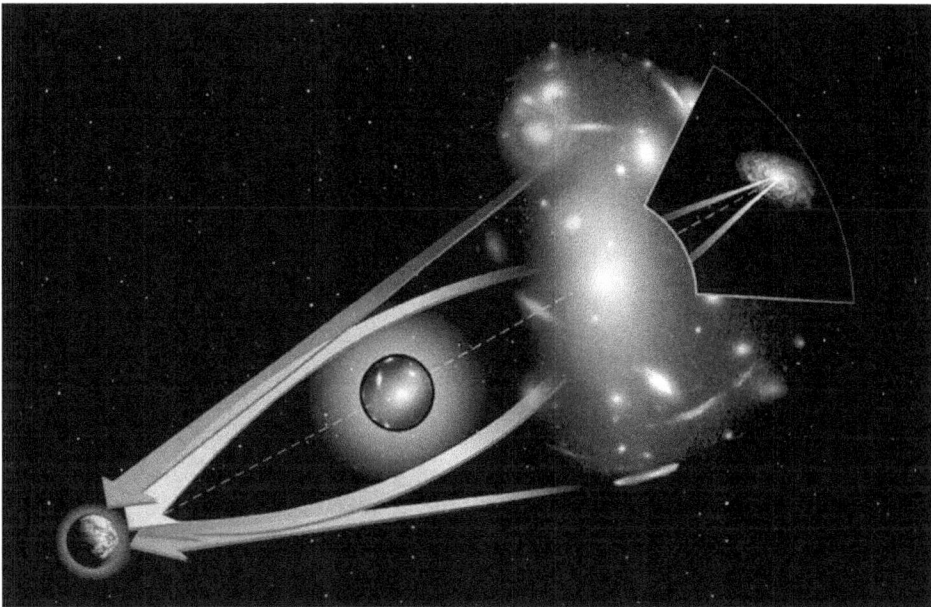

Graphic depiction of the effect of a large galaxy cluster (center) on light rays as they travel to Earth (lower left). Inset shows the path of the light rays without the effect of the large galaxy cluster. Einstein's theory general of relativity predicted the effect of a gravitational field bending light rays. This was first tested during the May 1919 Solar eclipse.

Einstein is absolutely the only person who really captured what this is all about. And he hadn't full captured it.

And there's no difference between that and astronomy. True astronomy is in that. And true astronomy is not something that anybody knows, in a full sense. They don't. We have approximations. You get some people who are more clever, who have better practical insights, and so forth. But what we mean by that, is what we mean about the universe; it is exactly that: Mankind is not a creature inside the universe, as such. Mankind *encloses* the existence of the universe, that's the point. And the development of that enclosing is the progress of mankind.

Practical people are therefore stupid people, inherently.

We can deal with that in all kinds of ways. There are all kinds of aspects of what goes on in the universe, and you find that they all go together. *But!* The problem is that mankind has not yet discovered *how* all these things come together. Because they don't know the name of the thing. It's like Einstein,— Einstein made a discovery which no other person had made, never did. So therefore you can say Einstein was the only competent scientist, but he was not complete!

All the others who were not Einstein, were incompetent relative to Einstein. Because mankind is not something in some worldly universe, you know. Mankind is an integral part, the creation process of mankind; there is no real creation of mankind except in that way. In other words, mankind is placed in the universe, as such, in an explicit way. It's the discovery of what we can understand about this process. That's the crucial area. And Einstein went further than anyone, in terms of proof on that account. So relative to Einstein, all his rivals were incompetent; all their opinions were wrong because they were using premises of that type, and those premises aren't useful.

And as I have said several times before, it's the testing of the back side of the Moon, which is the best proof of it. The testing of it is right now the most significant thing for this kind of study. We don't know what the back of the Moon is! We know it's a happening, but we don't know what it is, what its principle is. We know we can get effects based on that, but we don't know what these effects are, as of themselves.

I mean, the proper thing to do, is say the basis of science is the name of Einstein. Because he did make a universal discovery, and no other person has done that.

Direct Insight into the Universe

Deniston: He made a few of them even. The revolution in science across the board from the very small to the very large, all centered around this guy's amazing work. It's really remarkable.

LaRouche: You have to look at it as a unity. What Einstein did was a unity, and the most crucial experiments that he did with respect to space make that clear. So the scientist must find out what the universal aspect is of the process, and test the principle. Because there is a principle, but you have to define what that principle is, and it's very difficult to define that, the way human beings work now.

And Krafft Ehricke had a mind that worked the same way. Most of the people who were saying they were followers of Ehricke, they were not really so. People like my wife Helga and other people, our people, who were working with him, were of his mind, but some of the others who wrote books on the subject, were not.

But the key thing is when you look at that issue, you find what it leads to,— it leads back to the Einstein principle. The Einstein principle is not something that is measured in numbers, and that sort of thing. It is something which *defines* the meaning of the universe! Or at least an improved appearance of what that is. But you don't discover the principle, that principle, by a mathematical discovery. There is no mathematical discovery which is competent for that purpose. But you

have to make, *create*,— create a solution for itself, and that's what Krafft Ehricke did. It was pure irony, when Helga spent time on this—and other people have done work on this—because that does open the gates for understanding things that need to be understood.

Deniston: I was struck that Jason found that Bertrand Russell in 1900 or earlier, had declared that the kind of space revolution that Einstein was later to create, would be impossible and could never happen— right before Einstein actually did it. So that to me was a very good example of the complete idiocy of the mathematical thinking, and the total evil of Russell's idea of no creativity and no discovery. But then it was completely thrown out, shown to be completely idiotic and absurd by Einstein, only a few years later.

LaRouche: The trouble is, it's not quite the same thing. Einstein's discovery was an absolute discovery. What he discovered was in the process,— was *his* ability to make those kinds of discovery. So you can't just substitute things. Because Krafft Ehricke had a very strong, accurate insight into this whole mess. Now Ehricke did not present that full program; Einstein did. Because Einstein went to the direct characteristic of the universe. Others went to an insight into the meaning of the universe, which is what Krafft Ehricke did.

Megan Beets: I think the state of mind that you're describing, Lyn, is the state of mind of a musician who's trying to apprehend the principle of a composition, and listening in for the essence of the principle of the composition.

What Is a Human Baby?

LaRouche: I think the word composition is probably a very poor term to apply to what Einstein represented. Because you're trying to synthesize something effectively, or as a way of defining the universe. But the point is, it works in the opposite direction. It does not become a practical expression of some alleged principle; it is the principle *per se*, not a model, or a reference kind of model which is relevant.

It's in Einstein's advanced work, his most advanced work in particular, that his method is something that *no other scientist*, as a scientist, has actually understood. And therefore, any interpretation of Einstein's method tends to lead away from understanding, that is human understanding, that if you accept what Einstein did, actually did, then you understand it.

In other words, trying to interpret Einstein is the wrong way. You have to discover what Einstein did, and then discover what the result of that is.

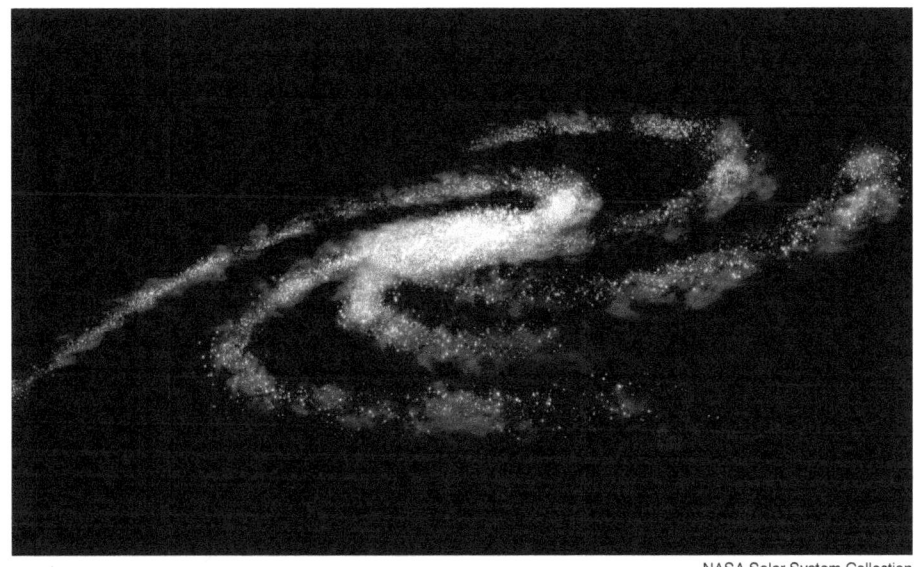

NASA Solar System Collection

An artist's impression of the Milky Way, our Galaxy, home to our Solar system and billions of others. The Milky Way is one of billions of galaxies in the Universe.

Look, what's the meaning of life? What's the meaning of human life? What's the principle of human life? What's the difference between human life as opposed to other kinds of so-called life? What's the difference? And that's where the problem lies. Einstein went with an absolute picture of the problem. His meaning is not completely perfect, but the conception of the conception is perfect.

In other words, if you avoid trying to interpret things, you eliminate the corruptions which prevent you from understanding what the principle is. Practical people are not scientists; they are amusements.

People should get into this, our people should get into this, just that point. You have to look at the most challenging thoughts of Einstein to understand what this whole business is all about.

This is the same thing,— you're doing a study in the Solar system, the Galactic system, and so forth; all these things are subjects of investigations, they are not truths. Einstein presents a distinction of argument which qualifies as truth; it doesn't mean he knows everything. It means that what he's done, his principle conforms to an idea of truth. And I think that likewise, the back side of the Moon is probably the best example to focus on, to understand what this whole thing all means.

The back side of the Moon! We can know the information that we experience of the Moon, but we have not understood the creation of the process by which this operation itself functions, because you don't know what the back side of the Moon is.

Deniston: Are you referring, in part, to the process of the creation of the Solar system as a whole?

LaRouche: Not the Solar system—no! The Solar system exists as a phenomenon. But it is only a phenomenon, it is not a principle.

Deniston: So you're looking for what is the underlying principle that created that phenomenon.

LaRouche: And that comes in the ability of mankind to *create*. Systems of creation. And that's what Einstein did, to a certain significant degree.

Look, what's the meaning of the birth of a child, as opposed to the birth of some other kind of person ...

Deniston: A Republican.

LaRouche: No! A Republican is a wasted experience.

No, the problem is, you've got to realize that the universe is something which is the primary existence in and of itself. We do know some of the prohibitions as Einstein presented them. We do know some of the qualifications which *dis*qualify what the conventional arguments are. We do not know the full circle; Einstein did not know a full solution. What he knew was the fact of a problem, which was beyond what he was able to account for. But he could account for the fact, the *effect* of it. And that's what the important thing is.

What is the effect that you think you're reporting on? It's not an object. It's what is the most universal kind of implication. You don't want to use any practical—*avoid* all practical assumptions about the nature of mankind. And that's the problem that we get.

Yeah, Bertrand Russell, that's trash. There's no good, there's nothing in it. It's degeneration.

But what Einstein did was come into an understanding, step by step, which led him to this understanding of what the meaning of the universe was. And that's where his program and functions became clear. *We can be clear about that kind of thing: We do not know what lies behind it.* The back side of the Moon, the experimental treatment of the study of the back side of the Moon, that's the kind of thing, as a beginning.

And also, what about babies? What are babies? First

of all, they are uniquely human. No living creature is tantamount to … [interruption]

Deniston: Jason and Megan had an experience with some babies recently.

LaRouche: [laughs]

Ross: Little angels, yep! Little angels: These kids that we were working with up in New York City.

You May Not Get the Answer

LaRouche: Which kids?

Ross: About 30 of 'em from about 10 to 14 years old. I'm not sure what to say about it. It was definitely an experience, seeing what kids are like these days.

Deniston: Megan and Jason were in New York, teaching in an educational program, and I got reports from them. I think it was interesting as maybe a clinical example of what's happened to education today, because they got a very good insight, it sounds like, of the state of minds of this younger generation, and it reminded me of your emphasis, for a while, on the degeneration of education. I think this was a useful case study to present to people as an insight into why we need to shift the educational program, if we're going to have a functioning generation in the future.

LaRouche: What I would think on this point, is that it's extremely important to get the Einstein view—you know, it's extremely important. Because without that you cannot really get a clear basis for understanding what this involves. So it's better to say what we know about mankind and human life, the existence of human life, and what *don't* we know. And Einstein concentrated on exactly that, by his scientific definitions, experimental definitions; what he achieved is unique. Nobody has done anything like that, in that way. It was his work alone.

And the reason is, that the people in general *are not* thinking. They're not thinking. They're trying to find some theory about some object, or potential object, as being the source of understanding what this is all about. That does not work. What did work is Einstein's ability to approximate, and define, what was wrong in the existing opinion. What you want to come back to, is the denial of that kind of opinion,— that works. And it gives you a question, a bigger question to deal with as the next step.

That is, what Einstein said on this matter is the best thing we have available. So you don't have anything to work on, from among contemporary people, to get the answer to that question. Because they say you've got to find *a* substance, or *a* something, which you then adopt and you screw it down and so on, and you finally get the answer. But that does not work. Because what you're saying is: I'm going to define something on one side, and at the same time, I'm going to say,— well, nobody knows what this is.

That's where the problem comes up.

Einstein understood this by understanding the need to *deny* what is called "physical science" today. There's a higher level that has to be applied.

And the best thing is to just go to Einstein's own definitions of this question, his most advanced ones. That will give you a clue. It will torment you sufficiently to get an inkling of a clue.

Deniston: His collected works, that's recently come out, right?

Ross: It's still in process.

LaRouche: What?

Deniston: I think there have been some recent releases and translations of some of Einstein's collected works, that haven't been available until recently. There might be some good material in there.

LaRouche: But you've got to find where the fundamental problem is. You won't necessarily get the answer. Because he's laid down various theories in terms of theoretical material, on this kind of question. But otherwise, he pointed to things which were not defined. But his work is the most valid that exists.

Deniston: It sounds like we have quite a task before us.

We Can't Know It Yet

LaRouche: Not really! Not really. It's actually removing a belief.

The problem here is the belief which people have. That's where the problem lies. And the continuation of Einstein's work in developing the universe, that's what the problem is. I go at it a different way. I go at it on the basis of the human mind.

Because the question is, what is the purpose of a human being? What is the purpose of the existence of a human being? What is unique about a human being? What's the definition of that uniqueness? That's where you lose the track.

And therefore, you have to go another Einstein step, as Einstein himself would have intended,— to go the next step, to find a next step, which corrects the error of what he's doing already. In other words, he comes up with an estimate, he presents an estimate as a principle, gives an example. A good example, a very good one. But then, he doesn't have the final answer.

What he leads to, is toward a final answer, but it's not delivered. Because mankind has not made that experiment. Einstein has made an experiment which defines the basis for the request for the experiment. That didn't happen. Everything of Einstein's work as far as I know, is excellent. But it did not complete the questions.

Ross: It sounds like a direction to move in. I'm not totally clear on everything, but I feel I've got a sense of how to move forward.

LaRouche: Well, there is no such solution as would be defined, and that's what the problem is. The problem can be found by the negations, in terms of what Einstein himself did. That works. But you have to keep doing the experiments. You cannot get a close experiment; you have to keep making discoveries. There is no predetermined final answer in this. There is a principle of answer, which I know; but that's not the kind of thing we're talking about here.

But Einstein of course is valid, as being the best approximation of what mankind has been able to discover in this direction. That's all. That's all you've got. It's all I've got, but I got a little bit more on this question, because of my own work. I know what the problem is, and my answer has been that the back side of the Moon is the current question for mankind to answer. Then you can get an improved answer, that way.

Deniston: Do you mean that once we start to get some instrumentation there, the new picture that will be presented to us?

LaRouche: There is no mathematical theory! There is no mathematical principle *per se*, which can have any dealing with this. And that's what Einstein understood. In other words, you cannot make a deductive solution, or anything like a deductive solution in those terms.

Deniston: From what I know about the question, it seems the far side of the Moon is going to be presenting things that we can't forecast now, because it's completely new territory. So it is going to be something that is actually new; new insights into things that we couldn't even,— all of astronomy has been characterized by such surprises.

LaRouche: To me it's perfectly obvious why we can't do that. Why we cannot know the dark side of the Moon; I know why we can't. That's the point. And the only way to do it, is to get out there. So therefore, you're going into it, of not some fixed principle. You're looking at experimental science! And Einstein actually operated on the basis of his version of physical science!

His way, not their way! And that's the difference.

So the point is, you have to say, "What is the next experiment?" And the teasing out of Einstein, trying to tease out Einstein, is a mistake! Because the whole thing involves something which is missing, and the missing thing is called, "Go and take the back side of the Moon!"

Now, how do you do that? Do you look at it from this kind of thing, or that kind? No! What you come to know is something you *cannot* know, unless you *go* to the back side of the Moon, which is unknowable at present. Mankind's progress has always been the question of getting to know something that is unknowable. And that's what Einstein did. And that's what we face right now.

So we have to continue the process of discovery, and leave it at that. And what you have is, that Einstein presented the concept of what was apparently unknown, and that was his physical principle. He laid out a physical principle which was an unknowable, and he was right, as far as anybody has known so far.

I think we should call for the second part, behind the Moon, the sunless Moon, because that will tell you what the stresses are, essentially, in trying to understand what is doing this. Now, if you want to get a discovery, you've got to do that.

You know, you had some experience with that kind of thing, with your work about the system, your deepest work on the system.

Deniston: The Galaxy work.

LaRouche: Yes, the Galactic principle; well, the only thing you could do, is to just say, "let's look at the Galactic principle, apply what we know about the Galactic principle, and then find out what it is that we can't yet know, as a knowable thing." And therefore you experiment,— as Einstein did.

Deniston: Yes.

LaRouche: Our problem, in general, has been that Bertrand Russell is all over the place. And those traces of Bertrand Russell get in the way of understanding what the discoveries of Einstein were. And he was never presented, fully. He was presented in a certain way, of getting to this idea of what is unknown; and what can you know from an unknown; what you can know about an unknown,— and that he did.

But the problem is, I think most of the people who studied some of Einstein's work, have not grasped what they themselves had come to know! It lies with the nature,— what is the nature of the human body? What is the nature of the human existence? As of itself? And that answer has not been formally presented.

Applying the Einstein Standard

Edited excerpts from the dialogue of Lyndon LaRouche with the LaRouche PAC Policy Committee on Monday, Aug. 15, 2016.

Matthew Ogden: Good afternoon. It's August 15, 2016; my name is Matthew Ogden, and you're joining us for our weekly discussion with the LaRouche PAC Policy Committee. I am joined in the studio today by Ben Deniston and Diane Sare, and via video, we're joined by Bill Roberts, who is currently in New York City; Dave Christie from Seattle, Washington; Kesha Rogers from Houston, Texas; Michael Steger from San Francisco, California; and Rachel Brinkley from Boston, Massachusetts. *And,* we are joined today by Mr. Lyndon LaRouche.

Right before this broadcast, we had a brief discussion with both you, Lyn, and Helga, and you both emphasized the central leadership role in the dominant dynamic being that of Vladimir Putin, in collaboration with Xi Jinping, to create a Eurasian system. Lyn, you called for the formation of a leadership group from within the United States to cause the United States to work with this new, emerging system being shaped by Putin and Xi Jinping. So I want to invite you to make some opening remarks and get our discussion going.

Lyndon LaRouche: What we have to do, when we're looking at China, we're looking at other

NASA
Earth as seen from the Moon in a photo taken from Apollo 8, 1968.

parts of the Orient,— we have to make certain kinds of decisions. Decisions which show exactly the united forces of the population of the planet—at least implicitly—in order to represent humanity as a whole. We can entertain people in different places; we can discuss things; we can handle the languages they're running up against; we'll probably deal with that, too. But the point is, we have to build a global system, implicitly, and what we're doing here at this moment is one of those things. It's a global system to lay the basis for the creation of a new system of existence of what the United States is going to be.

This is our effort. What we're getting in terms of Putin and Russia, and other leaders in the Orient,— this is all one thing. We know it really in our hearts and minds; it's only one thing. Like the question of the space program in general,— you've got to think as Krafft Ehricke did; and he did that, and he died. Now his memory is very important in this respect and in this moment in a very specific way. But he died; and he told Helga, my wife, when he was explaining that he was going to die,— and he said, the problem is "I've got two things. I can do what I do, and I can die by this other thing which has gripped me." And therefore, the memory of Krafft Ehricke is something which I think we ought,— particularly those of us who have known the United States—ought to keep fresh.

This is a sacred moment, in effect, in order to build up a foundation for man's role in space, for man's participation in what space represents, and looking beyond that as well. That's what we have to do.

We have to think. It's like the way people deal with other people. They look at them and say, "Well, this guy is a so-and-so. I don't like him too much. I don't like her too much." This kind of thing. But that's not the issue. The issue is, what has mankind contributed to the function of the species called mankind? That's what we

"The process of mankind is a higher one. It's the ability to generate and develop children who are geniuses in one degree or another, and therefore their existence becomes something sacred to all mankind. . . .

should be dedicated to, and this is a good occasion to do it. This is not the only place that dedication can be delivered, but it's a very good one to choose. I think this moment carries that particular implication.

What is the Door?

Diane Sare: I was struck in the Saturday dialogue, Lyn, when you referenced the principle, the work of Alexander Hamilton, several times in response to a number of questions, including in particular the question of the injustice that has not been addressed since September 11, 2001. I was reflecting on this, because the week before when I brought up the planned performances that our chorus is involved in, of Mozart's *Requiem* for the 15th anniversary of September 11th, you brought up the question of Mozart and his "criminally induced" early demise, and his commitment to a clearly profound religious belief, which you can see in his *Requiem*, his final piece. I think it's very important that we raise the thinking of the American people to an appropriate standard. And therefore, the reference to these individuals and their contributions—particularly Hamilton as an American—I think is very critical in this period.

LaRouche: I think the problem is that most people in this day and age, and beyond, have no understanding of what the meaning of all of this is. They come up with an explanation which is like having a key. You can put the key in the lock and open the door, but most people

are not able to open the door because they don't know what the door is. What is the door? The door is human beings. The door is what human beings can accomplish. Krafft Ehricke is an example of that; he actually opened a gate to the future. Now, how did he do that? Well, he said, "I'm going to die"; he told Helga that he was going to die. And I think he said the same thing to a number of other people. But that is what he represented.

This is comparable to Einstein; very few people understand Einstein. They make up myths about him and explain everything in terms of what he was suspected of doing, which was nothing of the kind. He was simply a scientist, but he was a scientist who had a reach beyond what other scientists had achieved. He recognized that the development of mankind is not based on babies— not babies as such. There has to be something else inserted into a baby in order to make it functional; otherwise, it's just a thing. It's a squalling brat, or something of that nature, and squalling brats are not really religious things or anything like it. But people go around and say, "I'm this. I'm that. I'm this," and claim certain things. But they don't create anything; they imitate something. They copy something, but they don't create.

The object of mankind is not to reproduce human individuals; the process of mankind is a higher one. It's the ability to generate and develop children who are geniuses in one degree or another, and therefore their existence becomes something sacred to all mankind— even when they're dead like Ehricke was. Because that value, that judgment, that insight into what the nature of mankind is—and mankind is not babies. Mankind is the creation of people, not babies.

What that means is, the child, for example, requires, in the course of life, recognition. "Hey, Mommy, stop this crap. Stop doing this crap against me. I'm growing up. I'm not stuck in your category. I don't know where I'm going, but I know I'm going someplace else that's going to be very important. I plan to take that trip and do it successfully, and produce the fruits of that trip." Therefore, instead of looking at what is the popular interpretation of how this works, you have to develop children into human beings—not just children. That's where people lose a lot of things in life.

Rachel Brinkley: People think the unit of measurement of economy is money, but what is it really? It's really human beings. Whether you look at that as an individual, because that's your source of new discoveries, or a family, because that's how you reproduce individuals; the metric is human beings themselves.

Parents and Children

LaRouche: Yes, well sometimes the child is better than the parents. Sometimes the matured parents, in the process of becoming mature parents, are incapable of producing geniuses. As Einstein emphasized in a very highly practical way and a very advanced way,— Einstein understood humanity, understood the meaning of the human individual. Why is the individual important? Not because he or she was the child of a parent; that's not the reason. You can get a bad parent very easily; it's very difficult to get a good one.

Ben Deniston: I've always been struck, Lyn, at what I see as just a remarkable convergence between Krafft Ehricke's idea of the Extraterrestrial Imperative and your work in physical economics defining the necessity of anti-entropic development for mankind. There's no steady-state equilibrium existence for mankind. Trying to maintain any fixed level of existence will necessarily lead to the collapse of society. This was part of the framework of his Extraterrestrial Imperative, that mankind always has to change the nature of his existence as a species and progress to new levels. And that necessarily takes us into space at this point. That is just completely convergent with your work in economics, defining the same thing but from the standpoint of anti-

entropic growth for an economy. We have to progress, we have to work.

And where does that come from, for our unique species? Where does that really come from? It doesn't come from finding resources; it comes from the kinds of things that Einstein gave to mankind.

LaRouche: The problem is that most people can't do that. Most people who are adults, leading people and so forth, they can't do that. What they're proud of is their children, or the hope of making a slave of the child, which is also another thing. You can get a puppy to be a child of that type; some people have done it.

The point is that a certain kind of personality, in the process of development, reaches a level of insight into the future of mankind that the individual generally does not grasp. And it's the discovery of the discovery which is the characteristic of the individual who is a real scientist, a real leader in these terms. Because the human individual is not the product of a parent; there are many things apparent about children, but sometimes that's not your child, it's not your child as such. Children of a certain good kind actually come gradually to look with pathetic sympathy on the existence of their parents and their family generally. They recognize that their family has been produced as young people, but the people have not come up to the standard of the possible, nor accessed the standard of the creative mind. That's what the problem is.

Our existence is to produce minds which are not practical, but minds which are creative in a true sense. And people who want to be practical have to pay a price; they have to accept the characteristics of stupidity.

Kesha Rogers: Einstein spoke of the scientist who was possessed of a sense of universal causation, and he makes the point that the determination of the necessity of the future is just as important as the past. I think that he really inspired this and shared this with Krafft Ehricke. The problem right now is that both of these great geniuses understood that the understanding of the world, and the Universe, is not just based on building blocks of what has already been determined for you, but what you're actually going to create. This is the difference in the understanding of what we have today, in the sense that society doesn't have an understanding of their ability to create something new, and to create the future in the way that Einstein and Krafft Ehricke did, because they lived in the future.

Most of society today, their basis of life, their basis of economics and understanding is "How can I get by? Life is determined by what I can gain for the here and now." That is completely different from what the real human identity is.

The Divine Spark

LaRouche: Yes, sure. That's exactly it; but you just have to look at it in the right way. The individual of this type who is important, is one who grows beyond the characteristics of the parent. In other words, the child, the young child, or whatever the particular child is, who has that, will always be superior in devotion over what the other children got through education.

"...To generate in the person of a living being the quality of creativity, generated suitably in the young, who become carriers of the achievements of genius."

Einstein was that kind of genius, and there was nobody else like him at that time. There were people who got to that. There were people in earlier periods of history.

But the problem we have, the source of the corruption which takes a whole population, almost any population, and degrades it to failure, is that "go along to get along" view of the world. The legacy of that nature is the thing that makes people slaves; because they believe they have to perform a duty of recognition.

We produce children who are not failures. How do we do that? You have to have the right parents; that helps. You have to have that kind of insight of a mission orientation, that you are not a person who lives because you have a habit, or because you have parents or these kinds of things. That's not reality! Reality is the aspiration which drives people to make discoveries in defiance of their parents. Great people always live in defiance of their parents. I know; I've lived that.

Ogden: In terms of physical economics, one way that this has been discussed, is that society as a whole must be able to not only just reproduce itself generation on generation on generation. In other words, not just a replication of what has been done before, but the creation of something entirely new, so that the next generation has higher productive powers of labor. A higher capability of mastery of principle and technology. I think that was the key with Alexander Hamilton; that was the kernel of the American System of economics.

LaRouche: Absolutely! That's exactly true, completely true. But the other aspect is, what people do today; they don't understand this issue. They don't understand what it means to generate in the person of a living being the quality of creativity, generated suitably in the young, who become carriers of the achievements of genius. Those distinctions are the important area. People become so stupid and so corrupt so quickly, so easily; like kissing someone's rear end, or kissing a reasonable facsimile thereof. That's what happens.

You've got a child who gets the spark, and the child who gets the spark will always use creativity for a purpose, as a purpose. The typical students in the universities don't know anything. They know what they're taught. And the whole society runs around, attempting to respond to the injunction, "behave yourself." Now, behaving yourself often becomes the equivalent of being a monkey. The point is, children have to be developed in such a way that they are a creative force with unique qualities. This comes to the issue of Einstein's business. Einstein is not concerned with *a* baby; he's not concerned with the case of *a* baby. He's concerned with what is necessary to induce creativity in the members of a population, a kind of creativity which is immortal. And that's what he did. He was still inventing things when he was dead. He was at it.

We have the wrong idea about raising children, because you're thinking about how to get a structure for educating the child; and that will kill creativity in *any* child almost. The child says, "I am not really a slave of my parents or anybody else like that. I'm independent." And, fortunately, I've been pretty much an independent person of that nature all the way through my life. What you have to create is not successful people; what you have to create is individual persons who say, "No, I'm not going to go that way. I'm going to go for the truth."

Sare: I think that's the significance of people singing in the chorus. It is very hard to kiss someone's rear end when you're singing Mozart, for example. And we've seen this process of development of people— many people in the chorus have expressed that they were surprised that they themselves could be participants in something that was so beautiful. They come in, and they realize they can be part of something that they had not imagined before. In a sense, it's part of this education, to get a population to the point where they could be capable of understanding what's necessary to understand, if we're going to survive.

Death Is Not a Factor

LaRouche: Yes, but the point is, Einstein lived out a form of life, an expression of life, which is unique to him. Because he was one of those people who *didn't* go along, who didn't submit, who wasn't influenced by corruption. And the rewards are, if people want to get ahead,— well, if you want to get ahead, the good thing is to duck before the chopper comes down.

Deniston: Einstein completely changed the nature of how mankind exists in the universe. He completely revolutionized what our understanding is of the nature of mankind's existence in this universe, how it's organized. And it's those revolutionary changes,— that's the substance of progress for mankind. It's not perpetuation of some tradition; it's revolution, it's shattering old ideas.

LaRouche: If you look at the works, the writings of Einstein, you'll see a remark done by his expressions, and it's of that nature. It's the idea of devotion to the future of mankind, where death as such is not a factor. Now there are people, of course, in history who had that kind of devotion. They're not depending on what's going to happen to them, as persons; they're going to

They don't understand what it means to generate in the person of a living being the quality of creativity, generated suitably in the young.

worry about what the effect is, of their having been a person.

Bill Roberts: I think this is why Einstein was somewhat concerned that people were creating a bit of a cult of personality around him. He was a little bit worried about that, and it relates to what we're doing with Mozart. In New York, we're finding a funny kind of response from some of the musical layers who, on the one hand, do not understand this as the sort of intervention to address the political shortcomings of the American population. And at the same time, they don't understand who Mozart *is*, to the point that they even deny that he was revolutionary in any sense of what his role was in history at that time, as if he were just this individual outside history and we have his music, and that's what it is. But not as a political, revolutionary figure.

LaRouche: But you see, Einstein is a different case. He lived longer. And Mozart was killed, murdered. Murdered.

So when you're talking about Einstein, Einstein's qualities were of a very special nature. This is the man who actually explicitly understood the future of mankind. And no one else has ever done that. No one else has recognized that mankind is not a product of a child as such; that mankind is a responsibility of a person to live out a function of the future. And it has to be that particular kind of thing. And Einstein is the one person who really achieves that, achieves it clearly.

Other people of course have had the same kind of things. Many people have the desire to develop lives in themselves which are better for mankind, and they will often rebuke themselves in that way, by saying, "I can't do that, because I've got to look at the higher levels for which I'm responsible." But then when you get a child, who thinks like a true genius, and Einstein is exactly that, then you're getting a different kind of case.

Now, what happens—which is a tragedy—is that many parents, and parental households, and schools, destroy the natural creativity of the child. And that problem, that effect, lives out to the point of their death. And their life becomes a failure for that reason. They say, "I've done this, I've done this, I've done that, I've done this; look, I've done all these good things, what're you talking about?" They'll say that, but that's not the issue.

And if you look at Einstein, and look at what Einstein did in terms of space, what did Einstein base himself on? Einstein based himself on a quality of genius. Genius is something which grows, which is unstoppable, which does not depend upon being educated. And that's what Einstein did.

Einstein conceived the intrinsic nature of the Solar system, and nobody else ever understood that in that way. That's the difference. Now, yes, can we create people who meet those qualifications? Sure we can! Be the parent of the right child.

The Truth about Mankind

Dave Christie: Lyn, I think the question of what you just raised around the education system crushing the genius out of children, I think it could go the other way, too. I think that there's often an idea that genius is just simply a kind of phenomenon, and the role of culture is little understood in actually functioning to promote and develop a field of activity by which the individuals can attain genius. And I think the question of culture goes to what Matt discussed earlier around the extended reproduction of man, and that actually becomes the unit of what your economy should be, as Rachel said.

Because of monetarism, people oftentimes think of the unit of value as money, whereas what you've done with your economics—the concept of potential relative population density—it's not just how many people you have, but rather, what's the vector of overall direction of culture and of your ability to think and develop future creative individuals, future geniuses.

And I know, Lyn, just as a point of reflection, this is the 15th of August, when 45 years ago, Nixon broke with the Bretton Woods system, which you had actually forecast. Against all other economists that had discussed the "built-in stabilizers" of the system, you had a certain sense of a directionality that you saw the economy going, and I think it comes back to this question of culture, this question that if you're not even developing a future capability, then you're going to run off the end of the cliff. So I think there is that question of culture actually developing the creative individuals.

LaRouche: You know, I always, with respect to my parents,— I never gave in to my parents, never did. Because I had a different road, a different direction to go. And all people who've done that kind of thing, have the same answer. They may give into it, give into the problem; which is for them, corruption.

What I've dealt with is no corruption. I refuse to accept corruption. And Einstein does it the same way, has done it the same way. There are other people, I mean, great people in life, in the United States and elsewhere, a few of them,— and they have a devotion to a mission. Now, it's not a mission of trying to give a little hand to somebody and hope that they get rich for that reason. The issue is, think about the mind of the individual: The mind has to think about what the individual is. The mind has to criticize everything that the individual wants to like. And I never have *liked* the kind of life I've lived—never. I've enjoyed fighting a fight, fighting a war, but winning the war. Look at me now! I haven't won any wars recently, not in that sense.

But Einstein understood the nature of what the future in the universe was. And you look at the final results of his work. He didn't discover *something*, as such. He *became* something! He had a saying, "nothing is true except what the universe presides over." And that's what he did. And he was still doing it, and people who were close to him, when he had died, saw that, that he had an absolutely unique characteristic. He was self-sacrificing essentially, but he wasn't *proudly* self-sacrificing. He liked his violin, he liked a few other things like that.

But no, the problem is, there are very few people who are not prisoners of their parents, of their parents' opinion. And that is the most dangerous thing that can come upon the human species.

You have to discover the truth about mankind, and when you understand the truth about mankind, even when you are a child and know that your parents are behaving badly, that is what the future is.

And therefore, when you're talking about the future of man's space, the *future* of man's space,— that's what Einstein did in his final terms! He had this recognition of that; you know the fact, of course, that he was Jewish, which is extremely important because of the victimization that he had to deal with. It was not just the victimization as such; it was his desire *not* to be like that, to be a different kind of person. And he was quite a different kind of person, among all of the scientists of his time.

And so, if you want to create a good society, you have to realize what a good society is and how it works. What you do, what you demand, what you urgently need, constantly, is opposed to what you say, "well, I can miss that." And you see the greedy person who has an ego, and the ego gets tough and is like "I'm tough, I'm a tough thinker." Why is he a tough thinker? Because he's a stinker! [laughs] In one sense or another.

No, the point is, Einstein understood that the babies are not just babies. The valid human being lives to create advanced life of the progress of mankind, for its own sake, which is what *he* actually did.

Some people try to interpret Einstein. From what all I've seen and my experience, apart from a *few* things I've known, it's not there. It's an imitation.

Why the Music?

Brinkley: That's the inherent nature of a child, that's why they always ask "Why"?—and ask a million questions. They are testing you, they are considering whether what you say makes sense. So you see that implicit questioning and challenging and looking for the truth themselves. But you also referenced that we don't have enough people doing this. Why? Well, one is this question of the Bush administration, the attack on the U.S. political system over the recent period. And this weekend you discussed, for example, the Clinton coup, and the attack on Clinton's Presidency, which had that effect on the U.S. Presidential system that people stopped speaking up, and that that was the precursor for 9/11, or it was that same process. So we've got to eliminate the Bush factor in U.S. politics.

LaRouche: When Franklin Roosevelt was dying, there was a change in the United States, the policy of the United States. And then you had the other thing which most people had known, ever since Franklin Roosevelt died, just the evening, his last discussion with two friends; one of them was a personal friend of

EIRNS/Sylvia Rosas

Einstein understood that the babies are not just babies. The valid human being lives to create advanced life of the progress of mankind, for its own sake.

mine—I was then young—who was one of my sponsors in all I did in the economic field.

The problem is that people are trying to find a way of progress which will enhance their role in life. And Einstein was not like that. And in that respect he's highly significant for what he was in fact. And then people who did discover, study, what he had been working on,— they tried to continue what he had achieved, after he'd died. And, at that point, a fading away came in.

You know, we did the space program, the introduction from Germany into the United States and into Krafft Ehricke's program, this is one of those kinds of things that has the quality of loving genius: That is, to love what you do for the sake of the loving of what you do, and for no other reason.

I've had a lot of fun with that, you know, because

I've been kicked around a few times, a few prisons and things like that. But you have to give up all these dreams, which are actually fantasies, and therefore, you want to find yourself, *in* yourself, something which is beyond yourself.

Creativity! What're we doing in music, for example? Take the music work we're doing now. What're we doing that for?! We're doing that to create something—what? What're we trying to create? We're trying to create something *greater* than was ever created before. And you use music, for example, composition, as a medium for that purpose. That's what drives you. That keeps you free from shame.

And we don't do that. We have people who have devotion, practical devotion of all kinds,— but it's very tough for them to hold onto that devotion. But Krafft Ehricke did it. My wife Helga had a conversation with Ehricke, because the whole group there knew each other. And what he said to her is clear. There are other people who thought they knew what Ehricke had done, and their opinions were not really valid. Even a book was written on Ehricke, and it was written by the wrong author.

No, you have to look at this from the individual responsibility to the collective responsibility,— its function is to know in oneself the instruments, discover the instruments which are essential for the creation of a higher quality of human behavior—to rise above everything that is popular! To achieve what mankind would otherwise never have achieved if they were practical!

Practical people tend to be stupid. They may know all kinds of things, words, and this, and this, and that, and so forth. But that's not the issue. If you look at the history of Einstein's life, into the time beyond his life, the termination of his life, and when the documents were presented of him by the people who had followed him, it becomes very clear.

But society requires leadership, which is not leadership in any bullying way. It's a question of saying, what is the purpose of my life, since I know it's not going to continue. And, therefore, you devote yourself to trying to create, in and of yourself, something which you think has a higher mortality rate, that is a good mortality rate. Most of our failures in our organization, for example, have run up against that problem—the devotion to the mission, not just *a* mission, but the mission of the future of the development of mankind, without regard to mere life mortality.

Ogden: Well, Lyn, what you called for earlier today was the formation of just that sort of a leadership group from within the United States, to bring the United States into alignment with what's happening now between Russia and China, what's coming out of Eurasia generally. And to craft it around that conception, based on what is happening in New York City—for example, we do have the publication of *The Hamiltonian* that's been hitting the streets in New York City—and I think this will continue to provide the rallying point for the crafting of that leadership group that you were discussing earlier today.

LaRouche: Yes. Yes, that's why I'm concerned about that subject now, here and now, to affirm that instrument, of intelligence, which is necessary to ensure a successful development of the powers of the mind of the individual, as most people fail to understand the good things when they're presented to them. And to have the fun of enjoying the amusement of having beaten the Devil. And you have left his imprint, on himself.

Ogden: Well, I think that's a good note to conclude our discussion on.

LaRouche: Okay.

Every Day Counts In Today's Showdown To Save Civilization

That's why you need EIR's **Daily Alert Service**, a strategic overview compiled with the input of Lyndon LaRouche, and delivered to your email 5 days a week.

For example: On Jan. 7, EIR's Daily Alert featured the British hand behind the pattern of global provocations toward war. Of special note is British Intelligence's role in instigating the Saudi Kingdom's attempt to set off a Sunni-Shia war. This religious war has been the intent of British strategy since the Blair-Bush attack on Iraq in 2003.

We also uniquely update you regularly on the progress toward the release of the suppressed 28 pages of the Congressional Inquiry on 9/11, which would expose the Saudi role.

Every edition highlights the reality of the impending financial crash/bail-in policies that would realize the British goal of mass depopulation.

This is intelligence you need to act on, if we are going to survive as a nation and a species. Can you really afford to be without it?

THURSDAY, JANUARY 7, 2016

Volume 2, Number 97

EIR Daily Alert Service

P.O. BOX 17390, WASHINGTON, DC 20041-0390

- British Crown Pushing War and Genocide in 2016
- Financial Mudslide Goes On; Monetarist Tyranny Gloats over Bail-Ins
- Moody's Downgrades Portugal's Novo Banco
- Puerto Rico's Default: It's Every Vulture for Himself
- Wide Glass-Steagall Debate Set Off Again by Sanders Speech
- MI6 Mouthpiece Evans-Pritchard Touts Persian Gulf Chaos
- North Korea Tests a Miniaturized Hydrogen Bomb
- Uighur Terrorists Found in Indonesia
- Foreign Investors Are Flocking In to China

EDITORIAL

British Crown Pushing War and Genocide in 2016

IV. Obama Supports Saudi War Crimes

YEMEN

Saudi-Arabia Is Killing People and Wiping Out their Cultural Memory

by Christine Bierre
Editor of *Nouvelle Solidarité,* for the Schiller Institute

Aug. 10—The UN definition of genocide is "Acts of war with intent to destroy—in whole or in part—a national, ethnic, racial, or religious group." Yesterday, the Saudi coalition restarted a war against Yemen which meets that definition: An attack against the Zaidis, an ethnic and a religious group that has been in Yemen since the Eighth Century, and against the millennial cultural heritage of Yemen.

The brutality of the war launched in March 2015 by a Saudi-led coalition of ten states against Yemen has already led—in record time—to 7-10 thousand dead and more than 2 million displaced. It is an illegal war, not approved by the UN, and has not respected any of the laws of war: 23 hospitals have been bombed, 30 schools have been destroyed, and children are targeted. A UN report, quickly withdrawn after massive pressure from Saudi Arabia, accused the coalition of having caused the death of 60% of the 6,400 civilian victims since March 2015, of which nearly a third are children: 785 children were killed and 1,168 were wounded in 2015 alone, i.e. almost six per day! And beyond killing people, the Saudis are also targeting the population's history, by systematically destroying the rich cultural and historical legacy of Yemen.

If the brutality of the Saudis is not a surprise, the full military support given by the United States, the United Kingdom and France to this war, and the complicity of the most important mass media which do not report the facts, is shocking. Beyond bringing dishonor to the populations of those countries, this support is also a war crime, a crime against humanity.

This article, based on the warnings set forth by specialists in Yemen at a colloquium organized at France's National Assembly at the end of June, should provoke an outcry against those policies of the "West."

Sana'a, the capital of Yemen.

Destroy a People by Erasing Its Knowledge of Its Own History

On June 29, Hervé Féron, a socialist deputy of the Department of *Meurthe et Moselle* in France, launched a strong attack on the shameful war led by Saudi Arabia, supported by France, the U.K. and the United States, against one of the poorest countries in the world: Yemen. According to international organizations, this brutal war has already created one of the worst, if not the worst humanitarian crisis in the world, with more than 70% of its 24 million population now threatened with death by famine.

In order to remove the Houthis—a Zaydi Shi'a grouping that took control of Yemen in 2014—from power, a coalition of ten countries supported by the United States, the U.K. and France, is waging a war of disproportionate violence against the Houthis which has resulted in more than 7-10 thousand dead since March 2015, many of whom were children and civilians, in addition to 10-30 thousand wounded and more than 2 million displaced. Saudi Arabia accuses the Houthis of being close to Teheran.

But it is not only the Houthis that are being targeted; it is also Yemen's extremely rich and millennium-long heritage, its historical memory. Air strikes, bombs, street combat, and the massive looting unleashed by this state of affairs, have already provoked immense destruction, notably in three sites classified by UNESCO as World Heritage Sites: the old city of Sana'a, and the ancient cities of Zabid in western Yemen and of Shibam in the valley of Hadramawt in the central desert of Yemen.

Making matters worse, the Coalition is targeting sites which are of no military interest, such as the ancient Marib Dam, the very ancient city of Baraqish, and the regional museum of Dhamar, confirming the thesis that there is a desire to destroy the culture of an entire people. One single bombing sufficed to destroy the totality of the 12,500 pieces at the Dhamar Museum, stated Mrs. Iris Gerlach of the German Archeological Institute. Among them were objects of the Himyarite civilization (275 to 571 AD); hundreds of inscriptions in Sabatean—the language of the Kingdom of Saba (800 BC), and a collection from the Islamic period. These developments lead one to believe that the Saudis, who are Sunnis, are ready to do everything to exterminate the Houthis, followers of the Zaydis, a branch of Shi'ism. The declared objective of the Saudi war is to exterminate the Houthis and bring back to power Yemen President Mansour Hadi who had resigned.

To warn against the threat the war poses to Yemen's heritage, which is unknown to most people, M. Féron, in collaboration with Mrs. Anne Regourd, a researcher at France's National Center of Scientific Research—*Centre National de la Recherche Scientifique* (CNRS)—and at the University of Copenhagen, decided to bring together at the Bourbon Palace—which belongs to the National Assembly—the best world specialists in the historical heritage of Yemen in the areas of architecture, archeology, archives, manuscripts and music, which are often unknown to the general public.

There is no excuse for the behavior of the coalition. Italian archeologist Sabina Antonini de Maigret and French archeologist Jérémie Schiettecatte, joined Iris Gerlach in drawing up a list of 50 Yemeni archeological and historical monuments for UNESCO, that should be protected as a priority, and that list was delivered to the Coalition in June 2015.

Space does not permit us to review all the very valuable material presented at this colloquium. We will concentrate primarily on the destruction of the architectural and archeological heritage, in the hope that the public at large will be particularly sensitive to those beautiful images.

We are very thankful to M. Paul Bonnenfant for having loaned us the photographs he took in the period 1975-2004.

Architectural Heritage

CNRS researcher Paul Bonnenfant opened the first part of the colloquium by taking participants "on a tour

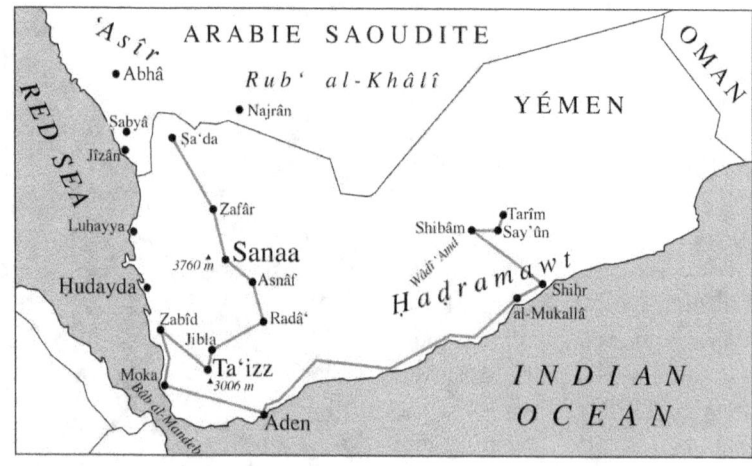

Map of Yemen, showing the location of the three cities that UNESCO has designated as World Heritage sites: Zabid, Sana'a, and Shibam.

photo: © Paul Bonnenfant

Fig. 1 City of Saada. Grand Mosque and Mausoleums of al-Hâdî Yahyâ ibn al-Husayn, the first Zaydite Imam from Yemen, who died in 910.

Fig. 2 Two views of Al-Hadi Mosque, partially destroyed by bombardments.

showing the effects of the war and the destruction of Yemen's architectural heritage" from the North to the South of the country. M. Bonnenfant polemically denounced the seven richest countries in the world for waging war against one of the poorest (Yemen ranks 194 out of 229 in *The World Factbook* in the list based on income). He also attacked the huge French sales of weapons to Saudi Arabia, "one of the most violent world dictatorships," and "denounced France for awarding its Legion of Honor medal to Prince Mohammad bin Nayef of Saudi Arabia." All that, he said, "is not very moral."

He began his presentation by describing the northern city of Saada, the Houthi bastion for which the Saudi's reserved a particularly murderous treatment. The 1,200 year old Al-Hadi mosque (Fig. 1 and Fig. 2) was partially destroyed by air raids, along with millennium-old houses of rammed earth and hundred-year-old minarets.

He then moved on to discuss Zafar, the former capital of the tribal Himyarite confederation (110 BC to 525 AD), the second largest archeological site of the country after Marib, which was also targeted by air raids.

He then discussed the magnificent city of Sana'a (Fig. 3), the capital of Yemen, which is one of the three UNESCO World Heritage sites in Yemen, where 5,000 of the 9,000 beautiful several-story houses of the Al-Qasimi district (Fig. 4), dating from Yemen's apogee (the Seventh and Eighth Centuries) suffered significant damage from air raids (Fig. 5).

He then discussed Radaa, with its Sixteenth Century madrasa—an Islamic school, and its aligned domes (Fig, 6), Jibla and the famous mosque and palace of the

photo: © Paul Bonnenfant

Fig. 3 The citadel of Sana'a, capital of Yemen. This very ancient site is still occupied by the army, and is at risk of getting hit by bombing and sinister collateral damage.

photo: © Paul Bonnenfant

Fig. 4 Houses overlooking urban gardens in Sana'a. Several of those houses whose façades lead to the urban garden of al-Qâsimî were destroyed by bombing runs.

Fig. 5 *Two views the al-Qasimi district after air raids. View on right shows bomb damage.*

photo: © Paul Bonnenfant

Fig. 6 *The citadel and madrasa al-Amiriyya of Radaa. This college-mosque of the Tâhirid dynasty (15th-16th Centuries) is very original in its architectural conception.*

photo: © Paul Bonnenfant

Fig. 7 *The citadel of Ta'iz which dominated the city, shown before the bombings. The several millennia-old archaeological site (the left half of the photo) was devastated by the bombings.*

Zaydi queen, Arwa al-Sulayhi, and Ta'iz, a city built on a 1,400 meter mountain (Fig. 7). At the center of the war during the last 15 months, Ta'iz has been devastated. Its medieval fortress al-Qahira (Cairo in English) was bombed and the museum destroyed (Fig. 8). The population of the city faces shortages of all basic necessities: hospitals, water, and food.

Other magnificent monuments are also threatened by the war in Ta'iz (Fig. 9, Fig. 10).

He then discussed Zabid, the second UNESCO World Heritage site. It was the capital of Yemen between the Thirteenth and the Fifteenth Centuries, and was of great importance throughout the ages because of its Islamic University and the

Wikipedia   photo: © Paul Bonnenfant

Fig. 8 *The medieval fortress of Al-Qahira in Ta'iz being bombed.*

photo: © Paul Bonnenfant

Fig. 9 *In Ta'iz, the madrasa al-Ashrafiyya, of the Rasûlid era. The Rasûlid dynasty (13th -15th Centuries) was one of the most brilliant in Yemen, especially from the standpoint of architecture.*

photo: © Paul Bonnenfant

Fig. 10 A Ta'iz, the grand mosque al-Muzaffariyya, of the Rasûlid era.

beauty of its civilian and military architecture, and planning (Fig. 11, Fig. 12, Fig. 13).

Finally, he described the old fortified city of Shibam, the third UNESCO World Heritage site, with its seven story brick buildings built upon the rocky spur of the Hadramawt valley. The impressive structures built in the form of towers contribute to the city's nickname: "the Manhattan of the Desert" (Fig. 14).

Fertile Arabia

Iris Gerlach is in charge of the Sana'a branch of the German Institute of Archeology. She opened the second part of the colloquium with a speech entitled "The Forgotten Arabia Felix,"

photo: © Paul Bonnenfant

Fig. 11 The Mausoleum of Aysa al-Hitar, in the coastal plain of the Red Sea, near Zabid.

photo: © Paul Bonnenfant

Fig. 12 The cemetery and the 'Aynât mausoleum in Hadramawt.

photo: © Paul Bonnenfant

Fig. 13 The very famous mausoleum of prophet Hûd in Hadramawt.

cc/wikimedia.org

Fig. 14 The old fortified city of Shibam, the third UNESCO-designated World Heritage site, is nick-named "Manhattan of the desert" because of its seven-story brick buildings.

Fig. 15 The vestiges of the big dam at Marib.

Fig. 16 Detail of a floodgate of the dam, damaged by air raids.

in which she discussed at length the archeological heritage of the Kingdom of Saba (dating from the end of the second millennium BC to 116 AD), reporting that today it is threatened by the war.

She denounced the air raids against the most remarkable piece of technology of that era, the great hydraulic dam of Marib (Fig.15; Fig. 16), which was key to the economic boom of the great kingdom of Saba, which extended from present-day Yemen up the coast of the Red Sea into Saudi Arabia, and across the Red Sea to Ethiopia, Eritrea and Djibouti. Far from being an isolated country, Yemen was fully integrated into the flourishing Silk Road which at that time linked the Mediterranean to the Indian Ocean and China. Gerlach continued:

> With the help of highly developed irrigation systems, Marib was able to transform the desert into fertile and luxurious land, and contributed for more than 1,000 years to maintaining the largest artificial oasis in the ancient world. A major crossroads of Arab commercial routes, Saba organized and controlled, in particular, the long-distance trade of perfumes, incense and myrrh. Those products, eagerly sought by the Mediterranean and Mesopotamian regions, produced enormous profits to the Arab Kingdoms of the old South, among which Saba was one of the most influential and powerful. That revenue was then invested, among other things, in the elaboration of construction programs of urban centers, sanctuaries, palaces and also water management installations.

Ancient Marib, capital of that Kingdom, was an urban center of 94 hectares (232 acres), surrounded by walls that protected magnificent temples, palaces, residential quarters, parking zones for caravans, and grandiose gardens. The gardens and the fields were irrigated by a vast system of canals fed by the great dam of Marib. That structure is a true masterpiece of engineering. The irrigation of the fields was possible because of the monsoons that arrived twice a year in the Yemen mountains. The precipitation was collected in the "wadis" [valleys, gullies, or streambeds that remain dry except during the rainy season—ed.] which fed the neighboring arid desert with great amounts of water. The large amount of water that would normally have flowed in a totally uncontrolled fashion from the mountainous region to the desert, was stopped at Marib by a dam built of two massive rock walls [4 meters high in the beginning, increased to 14 meters in later years, and 600 m length—Christine Bierre]. That barrier restrained the water flow and redirected it to rotary valves: the Northern and Southern rotary valves.

The Yemen Manuscripts

The third part of the colloquium dealt with the state of the archives, manuscripts, and the musical heritage of Yemen. Mrs. Anne Regourd, editor-in-chief of the journal *Chronicles of Yemen's Manuscripts* (CYM) described the wealth of Yemen's manuscripts and the need to protect them from the war.

In an article co-authored with David Hollenberg and published in the *CYM* (January 2016), the two specialists examined the specific content of that body of manuscripts, thereby contributing to a better understanding of the underlying reasons for the ongoing war between Sunni Saudi Arabia, and the Shi'a Houthis.

Compared to other Muslim countries, the Yemen manuscripts are particularly rich in the areas of jurisprudence, dialectical theology, grammar, history, *belles lettres* [literary works], science, Koran exegeses, and piety. They bear testimony to a classical Islam which between the Eleventh and Twentieth Centuries, produced a more "rationalist" dialectical theology, founded not on strict textual doctrines but on a necessary contribution from the intellect (Reason), philosophy, and logic. The importance of those manuscripts transcends Yemen as such, according to these scholars, extending to a cultural area which is a crescent including Iran, Iraq, Bilad al-Sham [Syria—ed.], and Zaydi Yemen.

In order to protect these manuscripts, held by many individual citizens, a big effort is already under way via a network of NGOs and nonprofit local organizations which are particularly motivated to do so. The different scholars addressing this colloquium underlined the extent to which the population of this poor country is aware of the importance of its cultural heritage, and goes to great lengths to protect it. The lack of funds is a serious problem, however, and these authors called for international assistance for those local institutions.

Call for Mobilization

Despite numerous denunciations, the destruction of Yemen's heritage has yet to provoke the general outcry that similar attacks provoked in Syria, Iraq or Niger. On Sept. 7, 2015 deputy Hervé Féron had already posed a written question to the then Minister of Culture, denouncing the "incredible inaction" of the international community. He asked the Minister to make a public statement aimed at stopping "Saudi Arabia from razing the several millennia-long memory of that part of the world" because, he said, citing George Orwell: "the most efficient means to destroy a people is to negate and to erase the comprehension of its own history"!

The French government has remained to this day deaf to those calls. We call on our fellow citizens to bring this problem up in the strongest manner with their elected officials at all levels, and to stop the participation of their respective countries in the ongoing genocide in Yemen.